Alexander Siedschlag

NATO Meets the Post-strategic Condition

Politikwissenschaft

Band 53

LIT

Alexander Siedschlag

NATO Meets the Post-strategic Condition
Political Vicissitudes and Theoretical Puzzles
in the Alliance's First Wave of Adaptation, 1990–1997

LIT

Die Deutsche Bibliothek – CIP-Einheitsaufnahme

Siedschlag, Alexander
NATO Meets the Post-strategic Condition : Political Vicissitudes and Theoretical Puzzles in the Alliance's First Wave of Adaptation, 1990–1997 / Alexander Siedschlag . – Münster : LIT, 1998
   (Politikwissenschaft ; 53 .)
   ISBN 3-8258-3853-6

NE: GT

© LIT VERLAG
   Dieckstr. 73   48145 Münster   Tel. 0251–23 50 91   Fax 0251–23 19 72

Distributed in North America by:

Transaction Publishers
New Brunswick (U.S.A.) and London (U.K.)

Transaction Publishers
Rutgers University
35 Berrue Circle
Piscataway, NJ 08854

Tel.: (732) 445–2280
Fax: (732) 445–3138
for orders (U.S. only):
toll free 888-999-6778

Acknowledgment

I gratefully acknowledge the support of a NATO Individual Research Fellowship in conducting the research that lead to the present study.

Contents

Chapter One
L'OTAN est morte, vive l'OTAN! - Fictions, Facts and Challenges   9

Chapter Two
Theoretical Accounts for NATO's Adaptation and Prospects   19
1. Beyond the Neorealist-Neoliberal Debate:
   From Metatheory to Praxis   19
2. Theory and Methodology in the Realm of Post-strategic Security   24

Chapter Three
The Global Dimension of NATO's Relevance, Role and Future   31
1. Theoretical Interpretations of the Causes and Effects of the
   Cold War's End   31
2. For an Existential Realist Viewpoint   36
3. New World Order - The UN vs. NATO?   40
4. An Episode: NATO and Out of Area   45
5. Global Factors Shaping the European Security Problématique   48

Chapter Four
The Regional Dimension - NATO's Institutional Adaptation   51
1. NATO's Institutional Potential and Adaptation:
   A Multi-Level Process   51
2. From 'Interlocking' over 'Interblocking' to 'Interacting'   60
3. The Mixed Menu of European Security - NATO Enlargement
   as an Example   65

Chapter Five
The National Dimension - Individual vs. Common Goods   71
1. Internal Linkages of Post-strategic Security Cooperation   71
2. United States: Multilateralism and National Prerogative   71
3. Great Britain: From Defense to Security   75
4. France: New Interests in International Defense and
   Security Cooperation   78
5. Germany: The Dilemma of Double Normality   81
6. Consequences for the Policies of NATO Engagement
   and Enlargement   84

Chapter Six
Alliance Engagement under the Post-strategic Condition 91
1. Euro-Atlantic Security Multilateralism:
   Path-Dependency vs. Mastery 91
2. A Final Word: What NATO Should Not Do 96

Chapter Seven
Conclusion and Outlook 99

Endnotes 107

Chronology: Hallmarks of NATO's Adaptation, 1990-1997 125

Bibliography 129

Chapter One
L'OTAN est morte, vive l'OTAN! - Fictions, Facts and Challenges

When, as the anecdote goes, the Nixon administration took over government in 1969, "all the data on North-Vietnam and the United States were fed into a Pentagon computer - population; gross national product, manufacturing capability; number of tanks, ships and aircraft; size of the armed forces; and the like. The computer was then asked *'When will we win?'* It took only a moment to answer: *'You won in 1964!'* ".[1] In the like manner, one could reason, compiling all the leading theoretical statements on NATO's state and future after the collapse of the Soviet bloc and feeding them into a 1994 or 1995 computer so to answer the question if and how the Alliance should enlarge and adopt new tasks, the machine might well have given out the message: *"Fatal error: NATO was dissolved in 1992"*.

Back to reality, however, with the Summit of Madrid in July 1997, NATO Heads of State and Government visibly set a milestone in the process of the Alliance's institutional adaptation. Inviting the Czech Republic, Hungary and Poland to start negotiations about joining the North Atlantic Treaty, they set forth a second track of NATO's adapting process to the new political and security context in Europe. That is, one of 'external' adaptation (in contrast to the continuing process of 'internal' political and military adaptation as rung in by the London Declaration of July 1990):

> Today, we invite the Czech Republic, Hungary and Poland to begin accession talks with NATO. Our goal is to sign the Protocol of Accession at the time of the Ministerial meetings in December 1997 and to see the ratification process completed in time for membership to become effective by the 50th anniversary of the Washington Treaty in April 1999. During the period leading to accession, the Alliance will involve invited countries, to the greatest extent possible and where appropriate, in Alliance activities, to ensure that they are best prepared to undertake the responsibilities and obligations of membership in an enlarged Alliance.[2]

Still, beyond the understandable focusing on Alliance enlargement and its ramifications, one should not depreciate the various other dimensions of, and pivotal issues relating to the future role of NATO and shape of Alliance politics. This is all the more essential as on the 'Enlargement Summit' in Madrid in July 1997, the Heads of State and Government tended to define the political challenges that NATO was going to be presented with in exclusive terms of ensuring a continued "open door" policy:

> We reaffirm that NATO remains open to new members under Article 10 of the North Atlantic Treaty. The Alliance will continue to welcome new members in

> a position to further the principles of the Treaty and contribute to security in the Euro-Atlantic area. The Alliance expects to extend further invitations in coming years to nations willing and able to assume the responsibilities and obligations of membership, and as NATO determines that the inclusion of these nations would serve the overall political and strategic interests of the Alliance and that the inclusion would enhance overall European security and stability. To give substance to this commitment, NATO will maintain an active relationship with those nations that have expressed an interest in NATO membership as well as those who may wish to seek membership in the future. Those nations that have previously expressed an interest in becoming NATO members but that were not invited to begin accession talks today will remain under consideration for future membership. ... No European democratic country whose admission would fulfil the objectives of the Treaty will be excluded from consideration. Furthermore, in order to enhance overall security and stability in Europe, further steps in the ongoing enlargement process of the Alliance should balance the security concerns of all Allies.
>
> To support this process, we strongly encourage the active participation by aspiring members in the [newly founded] Euro-Atlantic Partnership Council and the Partnership for Peace, which will further deepen their political and military involvement in the work of the Alliance. We also intend to continue the Alliance's intensified dialogues with those nations that aspire to NATO membership or that otherwise wish to pursue a dialogue with NATO on membership questions. To this end, these intensified dialogues will cover the full range of political, military, financial and security issues relating to possible NATO membership, without prejudice to any eventual Alliance decision. ... In keeping with our pledge to maintain an open door to the admission of additional Alliance members in the future, we also direct that NATO Foreign Ministers keep that process under continual review and report to us.[3]

This "open door" doctrine notwithstanding, NATO politics are far from sheer politics of enlargement. Many other, 'internal' aspects continue to have much politically explosive charge and impact on the Alliance's future shape and role. One concerns the role and deployability of the European members' forces in the face of newly increased U.S. interests in a re-balanced transatlantic burden sharing.[4] By the eve of the Madrid Summit, the question of enlargement had already ceased to be a genuinely *critical* issue. The finally successful candidates had long been treated as members in spe - for example, as hardly anyone noticed, sending de-facto permanent representatives to the North Atlantic Council. If enlargement was a contentious topic at Madrid, it was a struggle about numbers - inviting three or five -, whereas in less obviously spectacular controversial points, there were and persist deep matter-of-fact dividing lines between the allies.

While NATO's Madrid Summit was meant to be emblematic of the Alliance's take-off to a future of all-European security in unanimity, its overall balance was not so convincing. Having just agreed with Russia in May on a

Founding Act, the Alliance seemed eager to solve all the remaining issues in one big shot. Yet at Madrid, its member nations neither succeeded to draw a final line under the concept of reducing the number of sub-regional commands (from 65 to 20), nor did they manage to solve the struggle between the U.S. and France over the U.S.-led AFSOUTH command in Naples, with the latter demanding the next commander to be a European. It was also this struggle that heavily contributed to France not realizing its expected full return into NATO's integrated military structure. Moreover, not only were expectations disappointed but also new rifts opened up, such as a quarrel between Britain and Spain over Spanish air and maritime restrictions on Gibraltar, resulting in the British blocking Spain's plans to join NATO's integrated military structure until late 1997, which it had stayed out of since its accession to the North Atlantic Treaty in 1982.

At Madrid, it became obvious that the internal-political dimension of NATO's future was not going to be overlaid by the Alliance's coming geographical outreach. That is naturally not to say that expansion is not an important issue. In fact, the dominating *political*, as opposed to strategic, definition of expansion brings NATO close to its founding conditions, paradoxically. An expanding Alliance in some important sense is less bound to become a 'new' NATO than go back to its roots, if one will, resembling the pre-Cold War characteristics of the Alliance.

In 1948 namely, when negotiations about a North Atlantic Treaty were already under way, in the policies of the United States, Britain and France the belief prevailed that the Soviet Union did not seek hot war and thus there was no immediate need to counter Soviet military threat. Instead, the envisaged North Atlantic Treaty, at that time, when Czechoslovakia had just been overthrown by a Communist coup and a Communist victory in the Italian elections appeared likely, was primarily seen as a deeply *political* endeavor in order to tie the reestablished West European democracies together in order to make them less amenable to potential Soviet infiltration and the "Communist peril" in general.[5] It also was a first enterprise to reconcile economic growth, political stability and security in Western Europe, at the same time linking all of these to the North American continent. In this regard, arguably, it was to a large extent the Atlantic Alliance which sparked the process of West European political and economic integration.[6] Now it seems as if this development is about to be successfully reiterated in respect of Central and Eastern Europe as well as Europe on an all-regional scale.

However, as one must not forget, even fading out the dimension of enlargement and democratic outreach, NATO's post-bipolar potential for continued and even increased general functionality remains considerable. In contrast to temporarily prevailing radical interpretations, which either did not see any viable alternative and amendment to NATO in the area of post-bipolar

European security[7] or deemed NATO's raison d'être irretrievably vanished along with the end of the Cold War[8], the Alliance with its politico-military dual structure, as it has existed since its foundation, now as before exerts at least three key functions:[9] First, providing for the *collective defense* of its members according to Article 5 of the North Atlantic Treaty (in the face of continued but diffuse external threats). Second, fulfilling several *cooperative security* functions so to establish stable relations to its former adversaries on the soil of the erstwhile Warsaw Pact territory (in the sense of the institutional adaptation of its structures, for example by establishing the North Atlantic Cooperation Council, NACC, and the bilaterally-based program of Partnership for Peace, PfP[10]); this role also pertains to regional conflict prevention and management. Third, exerting important coordinating and cooperative functions *within* the Alliance itself.

On the other hand, diverse factors have indisputably amounted to cause NATO a loss of relevance:[11] The radically decreased public perception of clear-cut threats has posed increased compulsion to justify provisions for continued collective defense in the U.S. and Western Europe alike; the discussions about an own operational role for WEU and a genuine European Security and Defense Identity (ESDI) as well as the new activism of the OSCE have ended NATO's lead in questions of 'new' European security politics; extended early-warning periods and slashed military budgets have caused symptoms of free fall in some national force and defense structures, increasingly questioning short-term deployability of several national force contingents.

Unexpectedly however, exactly after the loss of its adversary and subsequent growing into different straining and controversial new security roles (like implementing UN sanctions or setting up diplomatic liaisons with the former Warsaw Pact nations), NATO has developed specific new legitimating potentials and moreover a remarkable institutional attractiveness - obviously reaching far beyond its mere self-preservation.[12] This not only has become clear in early Central European wishes for accession but also in France's "rapprochement"[13] towards the Alliance's integrated military structure. Just after the end of bipolarity and strategic security policy reflecting global interbloc confrontation, NATO is on the way of developing a considerable extent of independent, corporate identity (or, at least, the governments of its member states are prepared - for what reasons ever - to concede it a considerable extent of an own institutional action potential).

Also one of the factors leading to the Alliance gaining apparent corporate identity was the specific semantic character in which the discussion about enlargement had been conducted from its inception. Typically, the debates between the proponents of enlargement and its opponents did not as much center on the objective fact in question (that is, the increase in the signatory nations of the North Atlantic Treaty and a corresponding increase in membership of NATO's military and political bodies and organizational structures) as they evolved along metaphorical paths. Those "security metaphors" strongly conveyed the notion of an autonomous NATO as a coherent security institution and self-reliant international actor: the Alliance as an 'stability anchor', as a 'projector' and naturally evolving 'community of Western values' etc.[14] Together with the overarching "architecture metaphor" as it became the characteristic frame of the discussion about a post-Cold War Euro-Atlantic security order, this alone already caused an increase in NATO's institutional autonomy. No longer did national-power based geostrategic considerations or calculations in terms of the national interest furnish the chief points of reference in the public debates, but whole institutional "pillars", "bridges" and "cornerstones", with the Atlantic Alliance often regarded as the leading and integrating institution.[15]

Considering all these developments, the leading assumption of the present study is that the condition of the 'new' Europe, in its consequences for the future role of the Atlantic Alliance, means more than (and in part something different from) what it is commonly conceived of to be. The subject matter of the subsequent analysis is NATO's adaptation between 1990 and mid-1997, in the wage of the changed international and European setting after the threshold of 1989-90. Also after the Madrid Summit, related issues continue to have a strong impact on NATO and Atlantic Alliance politics. NATO enlargement does not terminate their relevance. As suggested above, it opens up a second wave and track in shaping NATO's future, but the first track remains, and it remains critical.

This study argues that one set of crucial factors determining NATO's future lies in the intra-Alliance political relationships in the face of the continuing prevalence of national interest-calculations on the side of its members, especially as far as common engagement in peace operations is concerned. The truly immediate challenges which the Atlantic Alliance is and will be facing not so much stem from external factors and from undertaking enlargement but from conflicts of internal origin, such as reconciling divergent approaches among its members to defense and security in the post-strategic realm.

That suggests not to limit the analysis of NATO's institutional adaptation and future role to its obvious immediate political context, the Euro-regional setting, but also to delve into the national context of Alliance politics. On the other hand, it is necessary to appreciate the broader context of post-Cold War international relations and security as the constitutive context for the distinct European regional setting NATO operates in.

It may be worth stating explicitly that the present study is not about the Alliance's military-strategic adaptation, such as its new force and headquarter structure, with the reform of the latter only achieved after the Madrid Summit of July 1997, which marks the terminus of this study. What will be of interest here are the *politics* of NATO's adaptation and its changing face as, if one will, an international political institution. This of course also entails strategic and military questions, yet looks at them through the lenses of policies and politics.

Taking off from these underlying assumptions and focuses, some of which are to be laid out in greater detail below, the study will seek answers to the four following questions:
- What is the distinct character of post-strategic European and transatlantic security and security policy and what consequences follow for NATO's current and future institutional adaptation and functions?
- What are the related challenges for international relations theory and scholarly analysis? What is here the practical impact of theory in the sense of "foreign policy engineering"[16] and concrete political guideline-output?
- What are the critical linkages between different contexts of post-strategic Alliance politics and security (global, regional, national) and resulting predicaments or dilemmas in their consequences for NATO and successful future Alliance policy? Here the national dimension is of prime importance, for the critical junctures of problems most visibly materialize in national security strategies and Alliance politics and must primarily be dealt with on this level. Note that NATO is an *inter*national, no *supra*national organization. Its member states have full national sovereignty in their decisions.
- What are feasible possibilities of theoretical integration in the light of the results found? In addition, what could be a feasible framework for post-strategic European and transatlantic security beyond the, as will be seen unrealistic, vision of a comprehensive European security order and institutional structure?

At a closer look, NATO reveals and faces an unconventional agenda of challenges - maybe except for the particular nature of the European 'new' security 'threats' and challenges, which has by now almost become conventional wisdom: They reach from nuclear proliferation over minority problems, the Russian near-abroad doctrine with its ramifications and ethno-national conflicts up to conflicts implied in the plan for an all-European security structure itself.[17] Conflict potentials and scenarios of such kind notwithstanding, it is unlikely that we will witness in the short term any escalation comparable to the post-Yugoslav contingency which would thus call for an analogous resort to the Alliance's military capabilities and operational structures. By now it has become evident that the pivotal challenges for NATO are considerably different from strategic problems and questions of regional stability in the narrow sense.

Important to notice, both the variety of possible conflicts as well as the available strategies for regulation have developed in contemporary Europe to such a degree that no sensible predictions about actual conflict processes can be made just by conceiving of more or less abstract 'systemic' possibilities for conflict as derived from 'tectonic' structural shifts. Already as early as in 1988, RAND analyst Robert A. Levine went as far as to allege that the whole history of the Atlantic Alliance could be written as a history of its self-analysis rather than its strategic behavior vis-à-vis a common adversary.[18] Therefore, NATO's military and political appearance at a given time could better be ascribed to the struggle of different national interests and the comprises made so to achieve a common denominator for Alliance politics than - following a strategic-structuralist logic - to be understood as a reaction to external threats. In this sense, according to Levine, NATO has always been and will always be an essentially "subjective alliance", whose future perspectives must not be derived from solely balance-of-power type reasoning or considerations in terms of external challenge and Alliance response.

Confirming Levine's unconventional point of view, NATO has moved, in its concrete activities, towards an essential role in dialogue and conflict prevention. The classical all-European dialogue and prevention-oriented approach within CSCE, now OSCE, has in contrast adopted important operative functions, along with creating organizational features such as a set of special bodies and codified mechanisms for conflict prevention and de-escalation. Whereas the OSCE thus has been engaged in several subsequent changes in its character and objectives, NATO soon reached consensus about its role in post-Cold War European and transatlantic security, leaving its traditional functions more reaffirmed and amended than changed and redefined.

As will be delineated below, NATO's institutional adaptation to the post-Cold War landscape of European security institutions in the period between 1990 and 1997 followed a way from 'interlocking' over 'interblocking' to 'interacting'. The so often invoked concept of interlocking institutions under guidance of the Atlantic Alliance threatened to materialize into a functionally unspecified, more inhibiting than reinforcing juxtaposition of interblocking institutions. The Berlin Ministerial Meeting of June 1996 marked a decisive turning point, as it gave up NATO's claim to an ever-leading role in the interplay of European security institutions, turning to the new principle of interacting institutions - envisaging a coordinated interplay and well-defined functional sharing.

One of the major findings of the present study deserves notice in advance: The Alliance, in continuing its process of institutional adaptation and enlargement, should refrain from adopting too diffuse political responsibilities and claiming a too broad functional spectrum in post-strategic security politics. Rather, it should adhere to functional specificity. This of course does not mean that NATO should devote itself to seeking to redefine post-strategic defense and security politics into all-out war military strategy. In the post-strategic security realm, military aspects of security by far not only refer to classical war scenarios or military intervention but also play an important role in peaceful management of internal conflict and democratic consolidation.

As the analysis will show further, NATO's specific long-standing functions enshrined in the Articles 2 and 5 of the North Atlantic Treaty - that is, politico-economic collaboration and collective defense - have remained remarkably unquestioned and even been reaffirmed by the system-change in Europe 1989-1991. Important to notice, they have always included contributing "toward the further development of peaceful and friendly international relations" by strengthening the member states' "free institutions, by bringing about a better understanding of the principles upon which these institutions are founded, and by promoting conditions of stability and well-being." (Article 2, sent. 1) In addition, the North Atlantic Treaty has always encouraged its member states "to eliminate conflict in their international economic policies" and to seek economic collaboration (Article 2, sent. 2). Nevertheless, NATO's procedures and politics to fulfill these functions and realize these aims are to be redefined and where necessary redesigned due to the changed political setting and scope in and under which it now is operating. Primarily, NATO had and still has *not to redefine its functional role but its operational prerequisites to comply with it.*

The Alliance was the first European international institution to devise its post-Cold War agenda and political guidelines, but it also was, and still is, the one to be most preoccupied with its internal adaptation, its self-positioning within the framework of European international institutions and with reconciling divergent national interests, which naturally have changed with bipolarity abating. From such a vantage point, it is not in the first place the much-invoked 'new security threats' and the Eastern outreach that pose the critical challenges for NATO's future. Rather, it are issues concerning the 'new' NATO's final shape itself. They include:
- The question of a European pillar of the Alliance and the extent to which it should be complemented or paralleled by a European Security and Defense Identity with own, distinct planning and operational capabilities.
- The reform of the Alliance's command and control structures.
- The relative importance of and relation between NATO's military and political structure and bodies.
- Ending symptoms of a free fall in some member states' national defense structures and short-term force deployability.
- The general course of Alliance post-strategic security engagement.
- NATO's stance in the institutional landscape of European conflict management.

These types of challenges mainly stem from a particular set of all-regional developments in post-Cold War Europe towards a condition of *post-strategic security* (a concept to be laid out in more detail below), which in the first place comprise the following:

(1) A *strategic de-coupling* of Europe: The reduction of its immediate dependency on both U.S. and Russian politics as well as U.S.-Russian relations and a resulting further loss of the extraposed stance of Europe in world affairs.

(2) Less allowance for *de-coupling of security issues form general political trends*, with increasing linkages between security/defense policy and political integration in general being even intentionally established. For example, political integration finds itself supplemented by an own security component (as in the case of an envisaged defense component of the European Union), or military integration also serves genuine political aims. This becomes obvious in the concept of Combined Joint Task Force Headquarters, entailing important political functions such as connecting NATO and WEU or providing a framework for security cooperation with East European states.

(3) Security (politics) in Europe is becoming *post-spatial*, increasingly influenced by sub-regional and transnational aspects (for example ethno-national tensions, separational conflicts, minority conflicts). This should lead to a broader security concept, within which security politics, conflict management and peaceful settlement of conflict are no longer contrary but complementary to each other. On the other hand, it must not be forgotten that geostrategic calculations, or at least rhetorics, still play a role. This becomes already clear in the Russian concept of the 'near abroad' as well as in a relative hyperactivity in the former Soviet bloc's rim areas. It was most obvious in the wars of Yugoslav succession but also applies, if to a lower degree, to the general political sphere of the post-World War I cordon-sanitaire nations' descendants, such as the Visegrad countries.

(4) The new Europe does not face the need of an *avoiding* strategy any more (avoiding inter-bloc clashes etc.), but in contrast it becomes necessary to establish *enabling* conditions, under which transformation and innovation can be guaranteed.

Chapter Two
Theoretical Accounts for NATO's Adaptation and Prospects

1. Beyond the Neorealist-Neoliberal Debate: From Metatheory to Praxis

Whereas the general theoretical lessons of the international-political change of 1989-90 are still being discussed controversially but at least seem to be sufficiently defined by now,[1] conceptual hubbub still as before prevails as for the question of the future of international security politics and the idea of international security itself. What precisely are the connotations of 'security'? - Is it more a political aim, an issue area, a mere analytical concept, a research agenda or a special discipline of International Relations?[2] Or can 'security' not be defined but in relational terms, depending on the respective system of reference and its specific problématique and causal nexuses, for example as 'national', 'international', 'societal' or 'global' security?[3]

Given their largely metatheoretical and philosophy-inspired character, it should not come too much as a surprise if the recent attempts to come to theoretical and methodical terms with the changed world-political setting rather will bring political science in still more disrepute with political decision-makers and their staff. Yet one must not forget that every politics have their implicit theoretical background, which also makes theory ubiquitous in international relations and security politics, even if some seek to actively reject it as hardly useful, distracting or disavowed due to its alleged failure to predict or explain the end of the Cold War. Namely, all reasoning about the theory-practice "gap"[4] in the study of international politics aside, the two have always been and will always be intertwined - willingly or not and for the better or worse, as Fred Halliday has illustrated so aptly:

> The difficulty is that the very pressure of international issues, and the demand for analysis and commentary on them, can act not only as a stimulant and a corrective of academic thinking, but also as a warp; the result is that not only the curiosity of the outside world, but the very work undertaken in universities is shaped by what funders and policy-makers read in the morning papers. To determine the academic agenda of International Relations by such concerns is, however, dangerous, not only for the loss of independence but also for the loss of perspective, historical and conceptual. Economists are happy to comment on, and be consulted about, the future of the stock exchange or the rate of inflation, just as political scientists can proffer a view on the outcome of the next election: this is not, any more than it should be in the case of International Relations, the basis of what they teach in a university.[5]

Even mere 'narrative' International Relations and security studies will never entirely escape theory, assert James Lee Ray and Bruce Russett:

Since human beings cannot be totally objective, even the most seemingly innocuous descriptive observations about international politics are 'theory-laden'. Consider the assertion that 'Germany initiated the Second World War in 1939 by attacking Poland'. It involves anthropomorphizing the states in question ('Germany' and 'Poland') in a way which is not only theoretically based, but objectionable to some scholars of international politics. The phrase 'Second World War' is ethnocentric. It might, more objectively, be referred to as the second phase of a 'European Civil War'. To designate the point in time as '1939' is equally ethnocentric, accepting the Gregorian calendar as opposed to the Chinese or Hebraic methods of assigning numbers to the passing years.[6]

Once one accepts this inevitability of theory in international affairs and security, it is only a little step to acknowledging that not only questions of how to adequately 'explain' international-political 'outcomes' but also those of political modeling and devising or evaluating guidelines for political action should be addressed (and hopefully answered) by any practically understood science of International Relations. Though a genuinely social science, International Relations should be reluctant to immolate their conceptual foundations and theoretical reassurances on the altar of a misunderstood yearning for 'practical relevance'.

In consequence, it is to a large extent precisely in order to try to show the way back to the mentioned practical *policy engineering* that the present study seeks to gain a theoretical perspective on the first wave of NATO's adaptation, 1990-97. What matters for any theoretically sound account on the Alliance's development and future after 1989-90 is to devise an analytical framework that allows for conceptualizing from a dual perspective the process of change which the Atlantic Alliance has been undergoing: Firstly, treating NATO as a self-reliant *institution*, that is, *as NATO*, beyond a mere conglomeration of its member states' interests and policy orientations; yet at the same time, secondly, heeding that the Alliance is no supranational institution, nor does it exist in a vacuum.

Though shaping an increasingly intrinsic-valued context for political action, NATO itself is again embedded in various other contexts. The foremost analytical consequence is to tie NATO and the process of its institutional adaptation back to its *constitutive actors*, namely the governments of its member states, whereas at the same time regarding it in the light of the *regional environment*. This environment is shaped by the new forms and conditions of Euro-Atlantic security politics as well as other existing security organizations, forums and initiatives in Europe.

These postulates, as will be argued below, can neither be met through a recourse to the currently dominant debates about meaning and effects of international 'institutions', as they are carried out between proponents of neorealism and neoliberalism, nor by bringing in assumptions of the paradigm of critical social theory or, as it has recently been proposed, utilizing concepts out of organizational analysis. Rather, it will be maintained, an adequate conceptualization of NATO's institutional adaptation after the Cold War can only be achieved through a comprehensive, *institutionalist* frame of reference, which must not remain confined to the narrow limits of the questionable 'institutionalist' debates in International Relations but borrow from general institutionalism in the social sciences.

That way, this study consciously steps beyond the declinations of largely misguided institutionalist attempts in International Relations, at the same time opening opportunities to unite important portions of related competing neorealist, neoliberal and critical-social assumptions and propositions within an overarching methodological framework. Starting with identifying the shortcomings of the institutions-debate in International Relations, the present study sketches out a more promising frame of reference for analyzing institutional change. Following on from this, it applies this framework to conceptualizing the empirical case of the Atlantic Alliance's institutional adaptation to the newly emerging conditions of post-strategic European and transatlantic security policy.

Whereas some five years of scholarly inquiry into NATO's future after defusing bipolarity brought forth a variety of post-bipolar security philosophies and treatments of the whole spectrum of Euro-Atlantic security affairs,[7] now the issue of Eastern expansion seems to have swept away much of those deep-grounded general interest in NATO's development. As suggested above, the problématique of NATO's future and the outlook on a post-bipolar European security order is and will remain by far more than a question of enlargement. Both the public and scholarly focus on this one dimension of NATO's post-bipolar outlook risk to too much divert attention from some other, related or different, fundamental aspects of NATO's future and institutional adaptation.

Foremost however, it is indispensable to treat NATO (and its future) on the grounds of more flexible theoretical and analytical instruments than the current grand *neorealist-neoliberal debate*[8] with its popular recourse to stylized propositions about national 'cooperativeness' and its stability allows for. Paradoxically enough, institutional forms *themselves*, while the original occasion for the controversy, do not play a very prominent role in the current discussions but are only examined in their effects (as intervening variables) upon national interest-formation and rational state action: Do states prefer a strong or a loose institutional framework when choosing to cooperate? Do they prefer institutional arrangements with few or numerous members? Do they prefer issue-specific or generalized arenas for cooperation?[9]

What the discussion constantly fails to capture is the fact that strictly speaking, the related theoretical assumptions all focus on *state action* and that consequently questions relating to international-political forms themselves are, if at all, analytically amenable to them only with severe restrictions. Yet exactly among those international-political forms numbers NATO as an *international institution* - with its growing corporate identity and at least relative de-coupling from immediate effects of its member states' short-term calculations in terms of national interest.[10] Nevertheless, much of the neorealist-neoliberal controversy will still boil down to the celebration of a questionable *structuralist* approach to international politics and security.

For instance, neorealism of the style of Kenneth Waltz, the predominant core orientation of neorealism's proponents in their debate with the neoliberals,[11] still asserts the uniform reaction of the "units", or nations, to (always equally perceived) changes in the international-political matrix of power to be the essence of all international politics and security, as the keeping of each unit's international "position" in relation to the others is proclaimed to be the ultimate goal.[12] For Waltzian neorealism, or structural realism, the space between the global international system-structure with its anarchy and the single states, or units, is thus logically empty. Therefore, there can be no forms of institutionalized regional cooperation but only temporary "amalgamations", which come and go with the respective structural shape of the world-political global constellation.[13] Even those do not possess any intrinsic potential but owe their existence - and, when time has come, their abolition - to the "most powerful states in the system", which use them as arenas for settling their relations in terms of national power and interest.[14]

Consequently, structural realism, as some of its proponents frankly admit, regularly encounters difficulty when seeking to come to terms with international cooperation that does not take place 'directly' in the international system and between, and exclusively between, single states but within *institutionalized contexts*.[15] Neorealist alliance theory has attempted to elucidate that blind spot by switching over to asserting Waltzian structural effects *within* those institutionalized contexts.[16] Yet it is far from examining those contexts *themselves*, merely opening up just another inventory of their possible effects upon national behavior.

Paradoxically enough, neorealism's neoliberal challenge in its common Keohane-inspired version[17] typically exacerbates rather than alleviates these biases. Originally departing from seeking to slacken and amend Waltz-type neorealist structuralism, it was fast at taking over insights from new institutional economics into international relations analysis but stopped far short of developing a truly institutional approach to international relations. Instead, it continued to search for general world-political effects on 'the' states as such. However, in contrast to neorealism, it no longer assumes them to stem from the anarchical organization of the international system but from the degree to which international cooperation is - at least on a regional scale - "institutionalized".[18] For example, guided by common norms, rules, reciprocal expectations and the structuring effects of international organizations.

These institutionalized rules of international cooperation, as neoliberalism goes on to argue, help states to save on transaction costs and to avoid suboptimal outcomes of cooperation; that is, they defuse the so-called "political market failure".[19] All this leads neoliberalism to assume that these elements of institutional certainty will lead even strictly self-interest oriented actors to develop an interest in maintaining and furthering once established forms and arenas of international cooperation.[20] In the last analysis, neoliberalism broadly takes over the structuralist methodology of its neorealist counterpart: It examines regular effects of international 'structures' upon 'the' states (how those structures themselves evolve falls beyond its scope). Yet in contrast to structural realism, neoliberalism does not spot these structures in the anarchical organization of the international system but in international "conventions"[21] which states, each following its own rational self-interest, commonly establish and abide by.

A differentiated typology of the corresponding international institutional forms however does not seem to be of much interest, nor does a closer examination of *their* qualities, conditions of existence and development as distinctive international-political phenomena - and not just as products of and arenas for rationally calculated inter-state cooperation, be it on the ground of incidentally complementary national self-interests of enlightened, common interests.[22] Rather, international 'institutions' seem to posses the bewitching gift to materialize into anything, nevertheless strangely always exerting the same kind of effects and obeying to the same structural logic outlined above. As analysis may demand, one time convention-based systems of rules are declared prototypical international institutions,[23] another time a specific subset of them, namely international regimes,[24] and if required, also international organizations are convertible into institutions, in that they serve as organizing arenas for multilateral cooperation[25]. This once again underscores that also neoliberalism's analytical interest is not in international institutions but in state action. Institutions only count in their effects on national international behavior,[26] not as genuine entities in world politics[27].

Consequently, neoliberal analysis of policy or institutional change in international relations is not so much interested in how institutional forms themselves adapt to a changed international-political setting[28] as it is in the "*effects of institutions*" on the states[29]. International politics thus finds itself reduced to an endlessly iterated game of reciprocal adaptation of short-term national interests to some fairly common shared objectives such as avoiding suboptimality in cooperation. Neoliberalism is far from being an institutionalist approach, let alone the "institutionalist theory" it has been seeking to declare itself [30]. All it can claim to be, as John Mearsheimer remarked, is a theory of "*institutionalized iteration*" of inter-state cooperation.[31]

Puzzling of this neoliberal kind does not only miss political reality, which even in the security realm does not simply consist in spot decisions with instantly calculable loss or gain but in confounded payoffs of different, *intersecting* political 'games' and joint acts, that is, "conjunctures"[32] of at first sight seemingly independent developments. It also fails to incorporate, or possibly even notice, important theoretical insights beyond the cooperation-under-anarchy scope. For example, so-called liberal-intergovernmentalist research has shown that states not only jump forth from one bargaining spot to another but in contrast may use 'historical', existent cooperative arrangements to back their current bargaining position or to mobilize domestic support.[33]

Shutting itself off from those theoretical insights, the current neorealist-neoliberal debate, despite or rather because of its shallow institutionalist rhetoric, more hinders than fosters an adequate analysis of international-political forms, such as for example the Atlantic Alliance, which have grown beyond mere reiterated spots of cooperation. It has not much to contribute to focusing on those international-political forms *as such* and not abiding by examining them as mere structural arenas or normative standard-producers for more efficient inter-state cooperation. Moreover, the related structuralist modes of thought fail to capture the distinctive character of the international context in which both international institutions and states - in our case NATO and its members - exist and operate. And that is, in the present case, the new condition of post-strategic security.

2. Theory and Methodology in the Realm of Post-strategic Security

What only seems to have a chance of advancing theory and analysis in the emerging field of *post-strategic security* is concentrating upon the rapidly growing dynamic and interdependence of different political problématiques and continuous redefinition of political referential structures. The concept of post-strategic security contests the notion of traditional, zero-sum type strategic security as it dominated during bipolarity, with its clear bloc structures, well-defined and comparatively well-calculable actors and scenarios of crisis and threat. In contrast, the new era of post-strategic security, especially with a view to NATO and the new European condition, is characterized by a diffusion of actors, institutions and conflict potentials. At the same time, there is an obvious ameliorative transformation of conflict. This however is for the most part not a sign of an emerging congenial Europe because the essential dynamic of conflict has, at least for the time being, but sunk beneath the international level. Here it continues to exist and exert its effects.

In consequence, paradoxically, the currently most probable sources even of international or regional conflict are of intra- and transnational nature such as ethno-nationalism, minorities, migration or proliferation). In this regard, the texture of post-strategic security, what has luckily come to be a trivial insight in the meantime, firstly results from the vanishing bipolar pattern of world politics (as opposed to the advent of a novus ordo saeclorum). Therefore, the 'narrow', strategically inclined concept of security has given way to the often-invoked 'broad' or 'comprehensive' understanding. This again results in growing competition between different European 'security institutions' (NATO, WEU, OSCE and also the European Common Foreign and Security Policy, or CFSP, established in 1992), which in their activities as well as political claims have come more to overlap than mutually reinforce, let alone 'interlock' each other. Thus, post-Cold War European security seems chronically "underinsured", despite, or rather because of its institutional multiplicity.[34]

In contrast to strategic security policy as a procedure of deterrence and avoidance, post-strategic security, especially as regards the East European transitional space, will have to be a procedure of political development. Here at least, security politics have actually become genuine *politics*, beyond narrow calculations of military capabilities, bargaining, or strategies of immediate crisis reaction. The existence, or absence, of a common political framework will be the critical variable deciding about success and failure of post-strategic security engagement. This importance of politics comes in the first place from the fact that there is no immediately existential common Euro-transatlantic security interest any more.

This makes it difficult to translate the historically remarkable pan-European and transatlantic international value-consensus about the predominance of peaceful conflict management into a specific consensus both about the future organization of common European security and common action in single cases. Here, calculations in terms of the national interest, as the study will argue, clearly prevail over common values. In this sense, the condition of post-strategic security newly poses the classical question of alliance cohesion. That is especially important for the future of the Atlantic Alliance: Decisive becomes the allies' ability to agree upon general political guidelines and devise according genuinely *common*, not just incidentally complementary, interests.

The crucial theoretical and political puzzle then is the actors' steady *self-positioning* in the face of security trends and risks. This brings functions of theory into the foreground that lie beyond the scope of the neorealist-neoliberal controversy: not ex-post explanation but policy-escorting and projecting construction of scenarios. In contemporary international relations theory, especially the so-called Copenhagen school[35] devotes itself to the related analytical tasks - together with proponents of a modified structural realism[36],

25

who focus on processes of regional political configuration that may vary from one issue to another, thus foreclosing any chance to be conceived of in structural terms of sustainable cooperation or iterated games.

In this sense, it suggests itself to refrain from reasoning about the mere *condition* of international or regional security, directing attention to the *process* of "securitization"[37]. That means trying to identify confluents of the various political trends and attempts to build a European security condition - beyond the illusion of a rational-functionalist security constructivism, which both the neorealist and the neoliberal mainstream share to a considerable degree. Quite different from the point of departure that Hellmann and Wolf chose in their seminal study,[38] NATO's future under the post-strategic European security condition seems less amenable to a structural-systemic type of analysis (as they saw it exemplified by neorealism and neoliberalism) than to a multi-level approach combining different levels of analysis, from the international system over institutionalized forms of cooperation and the national factor down to individual actors.

Especially the paradigms of *critical social theory*[39] and *critical security studies*[40] have attempted to overcome the structuralist and monocausalist bias that much of the neorealist-neoliberal controversy exhibits. They underscore the socially constructed, contextual (as opposed to structural) character of international relations, security and alliance politics. Consequently, its proponents now and again engage in the debates over 'institutions' in international relations as sparked off by the neorealist-neoliberal controversy.[41] However, critical social theory does not open a viable path to overcoming the mentioned shortcomings in conceptualizing NATO's institutional adaptation. While making a big step toward appreciating factors such as context-dependency of political action and cooperation, the institutions themselves still as always remain epiphenomenal. Though progressively understood as constitutive conditions for national interests, national identities and state action, they even here are not appreciated as political phenomena of an own kind worth of being studied as such.[42]

Organization theory, too, although recently applied to the case of NATO's persistence and evolution after the Cold War in a manner at first sight appearing plausible and fruitful,[43] provides no viable alternative. At a glance, it seems all-obvious that NATO should be a predestined object for organizational analysis, for it is not only a 'simple' international alliance but supplanted by important organizational characteristics. As Inis Claude observed,

> In organizational terms, NATO is something new under the international sun. It is an alliance which involves the construction of institutional mechanisms, the development of multilateral procedures, and the elaboration of preparatory plans for the conduct of joint military action in future contingencies. It substitutes for the mere promise of improvised collaboration in the event of crisis the

... actuality of planned collaboration in anticipation of a military challenge to its members. It is a coalition consisting not merely in a treaty on file, but also of an organization in being - a Secretary-General and permanent staff, a Council, a network of committees, a military command structure, study groups, and liaison agencies.[44]

Yet much as it is undeniable that NATO possesses and further develops important traits of corporate identity resembling organizational features, these are not quite amenable to organization theory. 'Organizations' in its sense are characterized by well-defined membership, fixed membership figures, durably marked boundaries, internal role and status differentiation, hierarchy in authority and by behavior paths shaped by the organizational structure and imposed on the members. With its various institutional out- and sub-buildings such as PfP, NACC - now replaced by the Euro-Atlantic Partnership Council (EAPC) - or the concept of Combined Joint Task Forces (CJTF), the new NATO has no clear-cut membership structure and outer boundary, but both are subject to change from case to case, according to the context activated. Consequently, there are neither fixed general behavior paths, nor can one speak in a strict sense of an organizationally warranted hierarchy in status and authority.

Given all those theoretical complications, the question arises how, or if at all, International Relations scholars can hope to come to terms with the conditions and process of NATO's adaptation. The answer suggested here is: It is indeed an *institutionalist* approach that seems most promising - as long as it relies on concepts and methods that stem from general *social science institutionalism*[45] and go well beyond the neorealist-neoliberal debate about international cooperation and institutions.

Institutionalism as advocated here mainly comes as a *methodology*, not as a set of propositions or yet another new theory of international relations. It pleads for a "methodological turn"[46] in service of better analytical adequacy, not for an all-out theoretical one. Regarding NATO, what makes it promising is that it offers a frame of reference allowing for arranging some promising assumptions of neorealism, neoliberalism and critical social theory together and linking them with insights gained by general institutionalist thought in the social sciences. Moreover, an institutionalist frame of reference facilitates multi-level analysis. Far from conceiving of institutions in neoliberal substantialist fashion as mere intermediate structural factors or intervening variables mitigating between the effects of international anarchy on state action and international cooperation, it sees them embedded in - if not constituted by - various intersecting contexts (in our case, national, international, regional or concurring institutional), which may shift over time and from one situation to another, exerting variable effects.[47]

Such a point of departure provides the opportunity to treat NATO at the same time in its own institutional character as well as its multiple context-dependency - from the general international-political condition over the European and transatlantic regional system, other security institutions such as WEU and OSCE, the Alliance's constitutive actors, that is, its member states, down to creative acts by individual actors, such as single governments or even political personalities, for example NATO's secretary-general. Admittedly, also in general social science institutionalism, a gripping characterization and handy definition of 'the' institutional approach as well as the very concept of 'institution' is yet to be achieved. Nevertheless, over the years a useful inventory of institutionalist methodology and core assumptions has emerged. Following on from it, for the purposes followed here with respect to an institutional account on the Atlantic Alliance, three typically *institutionalist* assumptions can be identified: path-dependency, discontinuity and multiple causation.[48]

(1) Political developments are *path-dependent* -[49] not only in the sense of a tendency of once taken courses to persevere but in the first place in the sense of the dependence of current decisions on past. Consequently, not only (national) political action (as for example the social theory of international relations assumes[50]) but also institutional developments themselves follow the principle of *context-dependency*. Institutions not only form contexts for state action but are again embedded in larger contexts, which in turn influence the conditions of the institutions' existence and development.[51]

(2) Given this multiple co-determinacy, political change as well as political action under institutional conditions proceeds *discontinuously* and *episodically*.[52] Taken paths of development are regularly co-influenced by contingent events and needs to react to new trends on a short-term basis. Additionally, *individual* or spot acts (as for example undertaken by single governments or officials) - whether intended or not - may exert effects on *collective* institutional forms. In this sense, interestingly to notice, already in 1979 Waltz proclaimed the principle of the "tyranny of small decisions", which under certain contextual conditions can cause inconspicuous "'small' decisions" to trigger vigorous "'large' change".[53] Hence, it appears dubious to call for a new, rational-intentional *grand design* of the future of NATO or even the whole spectrum of European and transatlantic security policy.[54]

(3) The only rule political developments really seem to regularly obey to, then, is the one of complex *multiple causation*. This results already from the fact that not only present problem areas but also the respective institutional history influence them.[55] For example historical ideas, which despite changed conditions cannot be abolished - already for reasons of continued self-legitimization. As for NATO politics, this becomes best obvious in continued emphasis of the principle of collective self-defense (despite the unquestionable

missing of any clearly identifiable and 'personalizable' enemy, which this concept usually requires).

The subsequent account for NATO's adaptation in the 1990-97 period will look into the three main dimensions of NATO's institutional context already alluded to, which also form the chief determinants of its future development, as well as the future shape of European and transatlantic security policy. One obvious context is, of course, the *European regional system* itself, that is to say, NATO's immediate operational context as well as other institutional forms such as WEU or OSCE. Most analyses stop at that point and do not delve any deeper in the two remaining decisive contexts: the *international-political system* (as the global context of the Euro-regional political space) and the *national dimension* (as the constitutive and supplanting context of the Euro-regional political space and determining factor for what kind of actual transatlantic security engagement, or disengagement, as the case may be, one can expect in a medium-term perspective).

The global reference of European security and NATO politics denotes the respective constitutive context and localizes the regional European dimension within the global international system with its fundamental organizing principles as they also apply to any regional setting. The regional dimension represents, of course, the specific sphere of developments, challenges and problems that NATO has been facing since the end of the Cold War and that the present study seeks to conceptualize and explain with a view to evaluating and 'refining' related theoretical statements and political guidelines. To delve into the national dimension of NATO's future role is especially important when seeking to portray an image of likely forms of future transatlantic security engagement, also as far as conflict intervention and the use of force are concerned.

Chapter Three
The Global Dimension of NATO's Relevance, Role and Future

1. Theoretical Interpretations of the Causes and Effects of the Cold War's End

NATO politics, one the one hand, have at the latest by now become a genuine *political* (as opposed to a strategic-military) enterprise and, one the other, not any longer constitute a sphere comparatively distinct from the course of Euro-regional and general international relations. So it is necessary to understand the current state and problems of general post-Cold War international relations and security in order to appreciate the various factors influencing the regional setting and Alliance politics in post-Yalta Europe.

Examining this global dimension is not only necessary so to systematically locate the case in point here, that is NATO's condition and development, within its broader institutional context, namely the international-political system, but also to answer a decisive analytical question: What, after all, is the distinctive character of the post-bipolarized setting as compared to the Cold War? Coming to terms with this question is of prime importance in order to identify the conditions of departure that *any* post-Cold War European security order is to face. It relates to general characteristics of international politics and security that also leave their imprint on the European regional system and its actors, be they nation states or international institutions in a broader sense (see the table on p. 33 for illustration of the following).

Given the diversity of the field, it comes as no surprise that there is a whole spectrum of controversial answers, depending on which paradigm one chooses as frame of reference.[1] Now as before, the clearest marks are the (neo)realist[2] and the neoliberal view, sometimes also termed Hobbesian and Grotian.[3]

(Neo)realism with its principally Hobbesian view of political relations as defined in terms of and largely determined by alignments and the distribution of power identifies the chief cause of the Cold War in the trivial effect of super power competition, exacerbated by uncertainty about the opponent's next move and resulting tendency for misperceptions to emerge.[4] Against such a background, the structure of the bipolar order appears as built up by the quest for power and security and tensed by the ever-present security dilemma. Causes of the long peace, then, were the stable bipolarized distribution of power and the obviously functioning system of mutual military deterrence. (Neo)realism sees the current era marked by a transition to multipolarity, ending the Cold War, or bipolarity, but not really the East-West conflict. It regards long-standing basic axioms such as international anarchy and the secu-

rity dilemma, if in a qualitatively changed mode, still as typical of international relations.

One example here is the concept of "emerging anarchy", which assumes that the security dilemma has not gone but rather been exacerbated by the fade of the bipolarized Cold War order.[5] The Cold War, of course, mainly resulted from the security dilemma, but then bipolarity itself overlaid and mitigated it. Over time, institutionalized channels of communication and dialogue as well as common norms and reliability in reciprocal expectancies formed between the blocks. Now that this framework has largely collapsed together with the Cold War, a West-Eastern slope in political institutionalization prevails. In the Eastern area of low institutionalization, the loss of the Cold War "overlay"[6] together with the dissolution of the Soviet Empire gave way to the condition of emerging anarchy: After an abrupt collapse of a hegemonic order, neighboring groups (from ethnic communities up to whole nations) as abrupt become conscious of the fact that their future, and also the provision of existential security, has now fallen into their own hands, with the reaction of the 'other' being far less 'pre-programmed' and calculable than it used to be. This condition may be an important trigger in escalating and internationalizing not only ethnic conflict.

In sum, on the grounds of strict (neo)realist thinking, one should expect neo-nationalism and all-European instability to rise if no tectonic countermeasures are taken. Respective proposed policy guidelines center on some new balance-of-power politics, if necessary relying on institutionalized multilateral interventionism. Rigorous (neo)realists would therefore have recommended, and still recommend, NATO to follow a modus operandi of strategic response to the developments in Central and Eastern Europe, as opposed to a strategy of political outreach, diplomatic liaison or even enlargement.

Drawing from Grotian trains of thought, *neoliberalism* regards the extension and contents of (broadly defined) international institutions as decisive factors for international cooperation, peace and stability.[7] It attributes the causes of the Cold War mainly to an insufficient institutionalization of the anti-Nazi coalition after 1945, resulting in a whole multiplicity of uncanalized conflicts. Still, increasing regulation of conflict by common mechanisms and collective learning from crises made the Cold War stay cold. The current era, in the neoliberals' view, is characterized by the spread of enlightened national interests: After the fall of the iron curtain, opportunities for interstate interaction have tremendously increased. According to its axiom that the behavior strategies and interests of states tend to adapt to one another the more often that states interact in comparable situations (law of reciprocity), neorealism expects a trend towards long-term oriented cooperation, also in the security realm.

	Neorealism (general)	Neoliberalism/ Institutionalism	Global Governance	Normative Theory/ Internationalism	Critical Theory (Neo-Marxian brand)
Theoretical background; decisive factors for peace and stability	Hobbes; alignments and distribution of power	Grotius; extension and contents of international institutions	Kant; democratic national government; resulting positive perceptions	Locke; centralization and effectiveness of international norms	Marx; hegemonic ability to define the world-political situation
Causes of the Cold War	trivial effect of super power competition; misperceptions	insufficient institutionalization of the anti-Hitler coalition after 1945	question of the future world order after 1945	insufficient "coercive" effect of international norms; no strong "world interests"	possibility of great power politics; low degree of politicization of the public
Structure of the bipolar order	quest for power; security dilemma	multiplicity of uncanalized conflicts	competing value-laden concepts of order	dispersion of international norms	imposed construction by the superpowers
Causes of the long peace (during the Cold War)	bipolar distribution of power; deterrence	increasing regulation of conflict through common mechanisms	ideological moderation of the opponents	(no typical statement)	(no typical statement)
Current era	transition to multipolarity	"enlightened" national interests; long-term oriented cooperation	core conflict over different conception of (global) order resolved	trend towards a world public; increasing norm-compliance	erosion of traditional power-"texts"; lack of new legitimizing tales
Current coin phrase	end of the Cold War/ bipolarity	conflict transformation	end of the East-West Conflict	principled world polity; global constitutionalism	deconstruction of overdrawn contrasts
Expectations for the future	neo-nationalism; all-European instability	historic chance of conflict transformation	peaceful world of liberal-democracies	effective norm-building under an UN aegis	global social change
Proposed policy guidelines and the future of NATO	new balance of power politics; multilateral interventionism; NATO's future development as a contingent strategic response	transfer of stability to the East; issue-linkages; skeptical about enlargement (lacking political rule-knowledge in Eastern Europe)	world-political project of democracy; expand Western institutions; NATO as a sphere of positive perceptions and democratic norms	intensify the definition of and adherence to global norms; NATO as part of UN sanction-politics (i.e. a UN sub-contractor)	abolish the rests of the old, bipolar, world-political text; towards a dissolution of the UN, NATO etc.); realizing global social security

Main directions in the theoretical debate with related propositions and recommendations for NATO's future.

(drawing from Volker Rittberger and Michael Zürn, "Transformation der Konflikte in den Ost-West-Beziehungen. Versuch einer institutionalistischen Bestandsaufnahme," *Politische Vierteljahresschrift* 32 [1991], pp. 399-424 and Alexander Siedschlag, *Neorealismus, Neoliberalismus und postinternationale Politik* [Opladen: Westdeutscher Verlag, 1997], p. 218.)

The appropriate denominator for the international political change of 1989-90, then, is not the 'end of the Cold War' or the 'end of the East-West conflict' but sustainable conflict transformation and institutionalization of cooperation. Appropriate policy strategies would be a general transfer of stability to the East, for instance by building issue-linkages between different political problems and agendas so to trigger spill-overs of cooperative norms and procedures from one issue area to another. Notably however, such an approach needs to follow NATO's expansion with skepticism, due to lacking political rule-knowledge in the new member states, which may endanger the so far reached level of cooperation and ameliorative transformation of conflict among the 'old' NATO members.

Apart from the (neo)realist (or Hobbesian) and neoliberal (or Grotian) viewpoint, at least three other paradigms are of importance here, which equally challenge the Hobbesian and the Grotian one. These are the global governance (or Kantian) school, the normative theory of internationalism (or Lockeian school) and the paradigm of critical-'deconstructivist' theory (or, if one will, neo-Marxian school).

The *global governance* school[8] departs from Kant's thinking insofar as it takes the internal organization of the interacting nation states as chief factor determining the war- and peace-proneness of the international system. It sees *democratic* states constrained in their international conflict behavior and driven to peaceful interaction by two factors: first their pluralist domestic infrastructure which makes it more difficult to mobilize military capabilities and pursue an aggressive foreign policy; second the allegedly increasing orientation of democratic governments towards international norms and peaceful regulation of dispute.[9] Elaborating on the latter, it are reciprocal positive perceptions that Kantians expect to further decrease the danger of escalating conflict between (Western type) democracies. They see the prime factor leading up to the split of the post-World War II great power concert as it was established by the Potsdam Conference in competing value-laden concepts of political order (Western democracy vs. Soviet-type Volksdemokratie).

Still, in its view, the long peace during the Cold War was secured by defacto ideological moderation on both sides. With the Soviet Empire's demise, Kantians see the core conflict over the respective different conceptions of political and global order resolved. Thus for them, the current era is marked by the end of the whole (culturally defined) East-West conflict, not just its politico-military superstructure, namely bipolarization with its antagonistic alliance systems and inter-bloc confrontation. Following on from this, proponents of the global governance school now expect a peaceful world of liberal democracies to emerge, rendering full realization of the world-political project of democracy the first point of reference for post-Cold War policy. This is to be accomplished by enlarging Western institutions, with NATO making one important, but no paramount, contribution to a crescent sphere of positive perceptions and effective international democratic norms.

Normative theory, or internationalism,[10] starts from what could be called a Locke-inspired point of view: It sees the degree of centralization and effectiveness of norms (in contrast to Locke, obviously, not at the national but at the international level) as the decisive factor for peace and stability. The Cold War, then, resulted from an insufficient coercive effect of international norms and missing strong world interests overarching the two emerging blocs. The structure of the bipolar order, accordingly, was made up and maintained by a dispersion and depreciation of international norms and common interests. Whereas internationalists make no statement about why the Cold War then stayed cold, they now identify a trend towards a genuine world-public and derive from the thus greatly increased observability of national international behavior a tendency to increased norm-compliance and collaborative spirit. This could lead to a principled world policy, a kind of "global constitutionalism" to replace the anarchical order of power underscored by the (neo)realists as dominant organizing principle for international relations.[11]

Internationalism further expects effective international norm-building under the aegis of the United Nations. Proposed policy guidelines are intensifying the buildup of and adherence to a common body of international norm-promulgation, collective sanction politics against deviant states and reforming NATO to become a part of an envisaged global system of UN sanction-politics, that is in the final analysis, rendering it a sub-contractor of the UN. Characteristic of internationalism as a descendant of what classical realists called the "legalistic-moralistic approach to international problems" remains, drawing from George Kennan,

> the belief that it should be possible to suppress the chaotic and dangerous aspirations of governments in the international field by the acceptance of some system of legal rules and restraints. This belief undoubtedly represents in part an attempt to transpose the Anglo-Saxon concept of individual law into the international field and to make it applicable to governments as it is applicable here at home to individuals. It must also stem in part from the memory of the origin of our own political system - from the recollection that we were able, through acceptance of a common institutional and juridical framework, to reduce to harmless dimensions the conflicts of interest and aspiration among the original thirteen colonies and to bring them all into an ordered and peaceful relationship with one another. Remembering this, people are unable to understand that what might have been possible for thirteen colonies in a given set of circumstances might not be possible in the wider international field.[12]

Critical theory, in its version that could be labeled 'deconstructivist' or neo-Marxian,[13] sees international peace and stability as always superimposed by the dominant powers so long as no socially just international political community is established. After 1945, the prime factor responsible for this superimposition was hegemonic ability to define the world-political situation. In this view, the Cold War resulted simply from the then perfectly given conditions for great-power politics, which themselves mainly resulted from a low degree of politicization of the world public. The structure of the bipolar order, as critical theory interprets it, was little more than an absolutist construction by the superpowers so to keep virtually all other nations out of their game, but in as allies.

The Cold War thus, especially in contrast to (neo)realist interpretations, is not seen as a structural effect triggered by the anarchical organization of the international system and the bipolarized world-political competition but as a "fight for loyalties".[14] Like internationalism, neo-Marxist critical theory makes no distinctive statements about the causes of the long Cold-War peace but is very decisive when answering the question of how the current post-bipolar era is best characterized: As an erosion of the repressive traditional 'texts' of power and a lack of new legitimatory tales, amounting to a deconstruction of the overdrawn contrasts stemming from the era of East-West confrontation. What critical theory expects for the future is a wave of global social change sweeping away the tenacious rests of the old, bipolar world-political texture. This results in radical policy guidelines, aiming to dissolve both the UN and NATO and subscribing itself to an emancipatory endeavor of realizing global social security.

2. For an Existential Realist Viewpoint

Which of these models can now serve as a sensible foundation from which to precede when, as the global context of the European setting and NATO's future role, seeking to grasp the distinctive character of the post-Cold War world with a special view to security politics, conflict management and a continued legitimization of alliance politics?

On a world-wide scale, the regional conflicts broken out after 1989-90 show that the end of the Cold War, in terms of security politics and conflict management, meant little more than the dissolution of the *bipolarized* world-political structure.[15] Various conflict data support the (neo)realist bon mot that with bipolarity, global threat and the resulting danger of world-scale conflict disappearing and offensive capacities slashed, the world in fact has become rather more insecure than 'civilized' and stable.[16] For example, from 1989 to 1992 the total number of worldwide registered armed conflicts increased from 46 to 54, subsequently going back to no less than 46 in 1993 and 42 in 1994. Moreover, in 1990 as much armed conflicts were started as for the last time in 1963.

Dividing the numbers of armed conflicts registered in post-Cold War Europe into a late-Soviet Union period (1989-91) and an early post-Soviet Union period (1992-94), we find 8 such conflicts in the first and 14, almost twice as much, in the second. So even if on a world-wide scale the total number of armed conflicts seems to have peaked in 1992 and to be declining now, it would be rash to allege a general trend of abating violent conflict. Including low intensity conflicts (defined as armed conflict with less than 1000 battle-related deaths per year), the period of 1989-94 saw a total of 94 violent conflicts in 64 different locations. Thus there is little evidence for alleging a progressive civilization of conflict, as global governance and neoliberalism do. Such a tendency, moreover, would have to be a bottom-up phenomenon (cf. the neoliberal law of reciprocity in iterated interaction in similar settings). Yet it is precisely smaller, low-level conflicts that have not decreased, as one should then expect, but remarkably increased in the aftermath of the Cold War. In the year 1989, we witnessed 13, in 1992 22-23, in 1993 15 and in 1994 17 of such conflicts. Intermediate conflicts (in statistical terms defined by more than 1000 battle-related deaths in total and between 25 and 1000 in that particular year) increased from 14 in 1989 to 18 in 1994.

These empirical data suggest a continued appropriateness of (neo)realist thought in the realm of international security and conflict. An important other argument in favor of (neo)realism is that, at a closer look, the end of the Cold War has changed or erased far less of the fundamental principles of international politics as they especially apply to the field of security politics than it is frequently argued.

It should be clear that with the breakdown of Soviet Communism, manifesting in the dissolution of the Warsaw Treaty Organization in April and the Soviet Union itself in December 1991, bipolarity, or the Cold War, came to and end - but not really the East-West conflict itself.[17] This conflict has always been defined more in ideological than in geographical terms, and the Gulf War of 1991 as well as the war on the post-Yugoslav territory underscored the endurance of the related incompatibilities. Quite different from the 'deconstructivist' and commonsense endeavors in contemporary theorizing as well as growing political hopes of a continued positive transformation of conflict and crescent culture of democratic peace in Europe, political realism - in theory and practice alike - is far from being anachronistic and obsolete. Noteworthy, political realism in general is also far from being a mere rationalized apology of power politics. In contrast, with its classical emphasis on systematic historical comparison and inductive heuristics,[18] it not only offers an overarching theoretical perspective on the long-standing organizational characteristics of world politics, the most important of which have remained unchanged beyond the end of the Cold War, but also provides a useful set of rules of thumb for conceptualizing politics on a more lasting basis than short-sighted beliefs and hopes.

For such purposes, what has come to be called "existential realism"[19] offers itself as a good starting point. This existential realism purports a pragmatic consensus about those realities of international politics that are simply given (or existent) and to be commonly recognized if one seeks international politics and security as well as scientific and political reasoning about it to consist in more than longing to ad-hoc decisions and value-laden exhibition bouts over 'good' ultimate goals.[20]

Existential realism underscores that three axioms of the international systems are valid now as before: firstly its *anarchical* structure and thus the lack of any central authority empowered to act independently of and if necessary against the prevalence of national self-interests, secondly the consequent tendency for the actors to resort to the principle of *self-help* and thirdly the *security dilemma*.[21] Whereas commonsense reasoning nowadays will typically deny the continued political relevance of the security dilemma-condition, newer trains of conceptual research have shown that it not only still has its traditional significance but - after the vanish of the bipolarized structural overlay - also extends to whole new dimensions.

For example, as mentioned above, in the field of ethno-national conflict studies the concept of "emerging anarchy"[22] has been put forward to catch the effects of unexpected desegregation of different ethnic groups, which usually triggers primordial revival. To grasp this new quality of the classical security dilemma, consider the following: The 'new' security dilemma will become virulent and directive for political action, on any political level (from ethno-national up to global), whenever a hegemonic or predominant global or all-regional political order collapses rather abruptly. What is important for the security dilemma to take effect, then, is obviously not the condition of anarchy *per se*, but the special state of *emerging* anarchy: Neighboring groups (from ethnic groups to whole nations) become suddenly conscious (or their political leadership successfully attempts to suggest them) that from now on, they have to provide for their security themselves.[23] Such a conception of anarchy also matches well with the onset of the Cold War, when the common phalanx against the Axis came to an end, also ending the globally structuring element of the wartime alliance.

Quite different from widespread idealistic hopes and transfigurations, the security dilemma did not disappear together with the end of bipolarity. Arguably, it has in fact only become genuinely relevant again in the aftermath of the vanishing Cold War. No question that the Cold War was the result of the security dilemma, but then bipolarity itself overlaid the dilemma and to some extent defused it; among the blocs, institutionalized ways of communication emerged as well as specific norms of reciprocity and expectations. The precarious yet also in that sense formative structural framework of bipolarity receding, a West-Eastern (and partly also North-Southern) slope in institutionalization of general political and security affairs took over. On the Western side and the level of the high-level politics of larger states, there is enough institutionalization (or, in Goldman's terminology, "internationalism"[24]) to buffer up possible negative effects of a reviving security dilemma, but not so on the former Warsaw Pact territory. The Eastern bloc's collapse left no relying mechanisms for institutionalized dealings of the newly independent states with one another in situations of conflict and crisis. Therefore, the push of some of those newly independent states for immediate regional re-integration, namely into NATO, which consequently would de-nationalize their just developed own national security and military policies, well confirms (neo)realist assumptions - instead of shattering them, as some still argue.

Accepting the empirical and theoretical outset presented here, it follows the insight that with the end of the Cold War various things may have ended, albeit the danger of escalating and violent conflict. Anything may have broken out but perpetual peace. To make things worse, one will have to say that especially in the post-bipolar world, violent forms of conflict are on the best way to gain a continuing position in world politics. Above all, these are ethno-nationally based tensions and crises. It literally seems as if the collective ideologization of world politics during the Cold War now were to be superseded by a regionally, nationally and subnationally virulent thrust of ideology. The corresponding cleavages often run straight through societies. This makes it difficult to redefine them, or at least to protect them from violent clashing, by military means. NATO, and others, had to have this experience in the IFOR mission. In those situations, even mere blue-helmet tasks, such as the mid-term separation of the disputing parties, seem to be increasingly unfeasible as long as they do not have a strong and lasting military backbone.[25]

The three axioms of existential realism noted above have of course little to say about adequate specific styles of politics and strategies of international security and NATO roles and engagement. They also by not means limit the set of available alternatives to intervention and a new balance-of-power politics. Just as little does existential realism give up value commitments in favor of realpolitik-type calculations of immediate national interests. What, in contrast, existential realism argues for is a common denominator of the outstanding specific characteristics of the international-political system, especially as concerns the debates about appropriate future security policies and adapted international institutional structures,[26] so to avoid tedious deep engagements in protracted debates on principles with little output for guiding actual political action.

For existential realism, the question of value-based yardsticks for foreign, alliance and international security policy is all but obsolete. Yet it openly acknowledges that every, including its own, theoretical orientation, just as every political conviction however honest it may be, necessarily represents more or less narrowly confined, partial perspectives on the vast variety of political affairs. Following on from this, existential realism consciously and strictly refrains from high-handedly recommending normative concepts for immediate political realization. Rather, it asks for the practical preconditions for developing and sustainably implementing those prescriptive recommendations.

3. New World Order - The UN vs. NATO?

To a large part shutting itself off from existential realist arguments, the early post-Cold War security debate, from its very onset, had been dominated by hopes of an increased peace effect through renewed traditional international organizations.[27] Starting with anticipating a more effective global security system in the framework of a 'new' UN, now that the Soviet veto-policy had ended, then turning to high expectations in regional cooperation as exemplified by the celebrated promise of OSCE, the 'new' CSCE, it ended at the subregional level, focusing on the general peace-sobering potential of a 'new' NATO. The dashed idealistic hopes pinned on the 'new' UN to become the one and leading post-Cold War security organization, rendering all other security alignments (including the NATO) mere subordinated, functional subsystems are commonly attributed to its failure to come to terms with the Somalia humanitarian intervention and the Yugoslav contingency. Apart from, or possibly in addition to, these empirical discredits, a global and leading role of the UN in security affairs would already have been questionable from a legalist perspective. Looking at those determinants can contribute to a more realistic assessment of the prerequisites of and chances for multilateral international security policy and peace operations conducted by international organizations. The related considerations naturally not only apply to the UN but also are of importance for evaluating similar constraints on NATO's adaptation and feasible paths of development.

In the classical formulation of Hans J. Morgenthau, the founding father of the discipline of International Relations and one of the early heralds of realist theory, the outstanding characteristic of international law is the complete "decentralization" of its legislative and adjudicative functions.[28] Shattering much of the normative theory's assumptions, this means that there is no one central power to set, let alone enforce, compulsory international legal norms. Two fundamentals result, with which any efforts to realize any 'international order' see themselves confronted: Firstly, the law of nations owes its very existence just to the single sovereign nations because it only emerged from and only can develop in dependence on their interactions, and it needs their capabilities to become enforceable; secondly, international law constitutes anything but a world polity (as however normative theory maintains), for every state is only bound to those rules of international law it subjected itself voluntarily to.

International organizations are no autonomous, unitary actors in world affairs but alignments of states based on a treaty according to international law. And international law is not the law of an international community but the law of sovereign nations. Consequently, all international organizations and institutions fulfil derived functions, derived from the sovereignty and interests of their member states and are, therefore, clearly determined in their aims and activity. Member states do not lose their autonomous legal (and political) personality but in contrast only form an international organization through their own legal personalities, capabilities and authorities, which they may handle according to their national interests and calculations of advantage.

Even what has come to be called *peace-keeping* and in the wake of the change of 1989-90 sometimes been asserted to be typical of both the 'new' UN and a trend towards progressively 'civilized' forms of international conflict management was, and will continue to be, in its most typical cases rather an effect of specific great-power constellations and related pressures to come to terms with conflict despite concurring national interests on the side of the peace-keepers. In fact, a broad overview study revealed that peace-keeping has been a recurring element and conscious strategy of international conflict regulation at least since the 1920ies,[29] which makes it rather typical of the *aftermath* of large-scale great-power confrontation (World War I, II and Cold War) than the advent of a new era of world-political cooperation.

In the immediate aftermath of the breakdown of the bipolarized Cold War order, the United Nations were often seen as a resurgent Utopia of global-scale security politics, replacing regionalism and alliances. Yet soon not only the Gulf War but also the War of Yugoslav succession let this Utopia go lost again - lost to a security multilateralism whose global formative influence will in the first place be determined by national capabilities and interests.[30] It by now has become evident that no system of collective security within the UN framework will render regional security alignments and institutional structures obsolete or at least reunite them under the global umbrella of the UN. Rather, as not only the Gulf War of 1991 but also the cases of Somalia and Bosnia illuminated, any effective UN security engagement involving the use of military force will have to resort to the logistic and operational assets of either the U.S. or a particular regional security organization that has sometimes been so vigorously reprimanded for now standing and acting in obsolescence - and this is the Atlantic Alliance.

The Alliance not only unites the nations whose participation in international peace operations has often enough proved crucial for its success. It also is the only working security system in the contemporary world. In a few aspects, its record may appear to some as ambivalent, for it could not prevent a war and recurrent conflict between two of its members, Greece and Turkey, and has had some difficulty in positioning itself in the new post-Cold War setting of European international institutions, involving a sometimes confusing change in self-ascribed 'new' functions (reaching, for example, from an out-of-area operation agency over a regional stability-projector to an UN sanction-implementation service). Yet it has indisputably reached an outstanding level of representing, in the sense of Karl Deutsch, a "security community". It disposes of a common military doctrine, permanent headquarters with international staff, multinationally integrated forces, a supreme commander for the Atlantic (SACLANT) and the European area (SACEUR), has always conducted multinational force training and maneuvers, and - which makes it even more unique in the world - it embodies effective common command and control arrangements, communication capacities and shared capabilities for transport and force-projection.

Considering the related national investments that were necessary to set up and maintain this security community, it is only logical that the Alliance, vice its official bodies, did everything to counter the view that the UN was to become the prime international security organization under the aegis of which NATO, at best, could play a sometime-complementary role and that decisions about common action within the Alliance must never be taken within the UN. Accordingly, then-Secretary General of NATO Manfred Wörner set out in his Venice speech of 10 May 1993:

> Despite its new-found authority, however, the UN is clearly unable to handle all the problems by itself. It simply lacks the military capabilities and financial wherewithal.
>
> Thus, in my view, we have to develop not only the UN structures but also the capabilities of regional organisations and arrangements, all the more so should the day arrive when UN cannot achieve consensus to act in a crisis situation. ...
>
> Already the Alliance's value as a partner to the UN is being demonstrated in Yugoslavia. We have helped the UN by providing it with detailed contingency planning on such issues as the supervision of heavy weapons, the protection of UN humanitarian relief operations, the creation of safe areas and the prevention of the spillover of the conflict into Kosovo. NATO and WEU ships are enforcing sanctions in the Adriatic. In recent days we have responded to the UN Resolution 816 and begun the actual implementation of the no-fly-zone. This represents the first time that NATO forces are engaged in a combat mission beyond their borders, and directly in a war zone ... I have no doubt that if the Alliance is called upon to do more, it will respond positively.
>
> Let me emphasize that these actions in support of the UN do not mean that NATO now sees its role mainly as that of a 'sub-contractor' for international peacekeeping duties. The Alliance, in the security interest of its own members,

is prepared to assist the UN; but it cannot commit itself to supporting globally every peacekeeping operation; especially where the conditions for success are absent, where it believes that the mandate and rules for engagement are inadequate, and where it cannot exercise unity of command. The Alliance's primary task will remain the self-defence of its members.[31]

When taking over office, also Secretary General Willy Claes was quick to embark on the position of his predecessor, stating "I should like to clarify that NATO is not a sub-contractor to the United Nations. We are a sovereign organization and ... in the final analysis, NATO's credibility is our most valuable asset. ... [W]e cannot - and will not - the credibility of this alliance to be squandered."[32]

NATO codified its strategic relationship to the UN in two documents, MC 327, entitled "NATO Military Planning for Peace Support Operations" of 5 August 1993 and "NATO Doctrine for Peace Support Operations" of 28 February 1994. MC 327 is a NATO military decision taken by the military representatives of the fifteen states in the Military Committee. French resistance prevented it from being approved by the North Atlantic Council, but it came to be used within the integrated military structure. In MC 327, NATO declares itself in principle prepared to cooperate with the UN but underscores that NATO decisions will remain NATO decisions and no command and control authorities shall be transferred to the UN. Most importantly, as a study cites MC 327, "national participation in peace support operations will remain subject to national decision" and the Alliance intends to use "its existing command structure ... to the greatest extent possible", with the details "to be determined on a "case by case basis".[33]

MC 327 does not specify any responsibility to report to the UN on the part of NATO force commanders, the North Atlantic Council or the Defense Planning Committee. The commander of a NATO-supported UN force will "normally be an Alliance flag or general officer, serving in an appropriate position in the integrated military structure."[34] This principle has already become practice in the operation Sharp Guard, that is the surveillance of the embargo against Serbia and Montenegro on the Adriatic, and the IFOR and SFOR mission in Bosnia. In the latter two cases, a prediction made in a 1994 study has proven remarkably matching the political reality of 1996 and 1997:

> NATO military thinking about the command and control relationship with the U.N. is likely to move in the direction of following the new U.S. peace operations policy. For traditional blue helmet peacekeeping operations NATO could accept U.N.-developed mandates and command and control relationships. These could be implemented by the NATO nations in cooperation with the Partnership for Peace countries. At the same time, increasingly restrictive policies could be implemented for mandates and command and control in operations likely to include combat missions or peace enforcement operations. Major

military interventions of the Gulf War-type might be conducted by NATO or U.S.-led ad hoc coalitions, based on weak and flexible Security Council resolutions. U.N. guidance would be limited to acceptable levels, guaranteeing NATO political and military freedom of movement.[35]

The Presidential Decision Directive (PDD) 25 of 4 May 1994, entitled "The Clinton Administration's Policy on Reforming Multilateral Peace Operations", well exemplifies this trend in U.S. national strategy definition as far as multilateral action is concerned. At the same time however, PDD 25 underlines some important regulations and restrictions that apply to U.S. support for UN peace operations:

> In improving our capabilities for peace operations, we will not discard or weaken other tools for U.S. objectives. If U.S. participation in a peace operation were to interfere with our basic military strategy, winning two major regional conflicts nearly simultaneously (as established in the Bottom Up Review), we would place our national interests uppermost. ... Multilateral peace operations must, therefore, be placed in proper perspective among the instruments of U.S. foreign policy.
>
> The U.S. does not support a standing UN army, nor will we earmark specific U.S. military units for participation in UN operations. ...
>
> It is not U.S. policy to seek to expand either the number of UN peace operations or U.S. involvement in such operations. ... Instead, this policy ... aims to ensure that our use of peacekeeping is *selective* and *more effective*.[36]

Other nations' 'peace-keeping doctrines' - as they will be treated in further detail below - make similar statements. In Great Britain, for example, it is an almost rhetorical question to ask what reasons there could be to take on any global responsibility within the UN framework but to secure one's own vital national interests.[37] As will be seen, Great Britain, like other countries such as France with its grande-nation tradition, has only just taken the step from defense to security - that is, defining its defense and traditional 'security' policy, also as far as military engagement in the service for peace is concerned, beyond a mere national towards a genuinely international focus.[38] Most remarkably in France, understanding of the fact grows that defense and security, already due to important shortcomings in national defense capabilities such as short-term force deployability becoming obvious during the Gulf War of 1991, no longer can be a national affair, but that in fact it can no longer be conceived of without international integration.[39]

Despite the political rhetorics and moral hopes of an uprising new era of *collective security* under the UN, the fact has been a trend towards seeking regional organizations as frameworks for multilateral peace operations. Here history seems to repeat itself, for the unexpectedly prominent role of the Atlantic Alliance in the new-type multilateral peace operations, which at first were widely deemed to do rather the last bit to make it as a *collective defense* organization, exactly parallels the setting of the upcoming Cold War when the hopes pinned on the just founded UN were already rendered unrealistic. As Inis Claude so astutely observed, then

> [t]he first reaction of the Western powers to the realization that they needed an arrangement for collective defense against the threat of Soviet aggression was not to reverse the San Francisco decision against relying upon collective security for this kind of job, but to create an extra-United Nations system - the North Atlantic Treaty Organization.[40]

4. An Episode: NATO and Out of Area

With the shattered hopes of a coming era of global collective security resting on the UN and executed through regional "special arrangements", for example NATO, the so-called *out-of-area* discussion[41] lost much of its energy and relevance. The question of NATO going, or going not, out of area on a larger military scale is an old one, accompanying the Alliance almost since its existence, and periodically becoming virulent.[42] This happened for example in the Suez Crisis of 1956, the Six Days' War of 1967, the Yom-Kippur War of 1973 and the Falkland War of 1982. To appreciate the causes and implications of the out-of-area issue, one should at first take a look at some relevant provisions in the North Atlantic Treaty.

The central regulation for the use of military force is found in Article 5. It is fundamental for NATO's character as an international collective-defense, but not a supranational collective-security organization and moreover still reflects its founding conditions at the beginning of bipolarity. The broad and somewhat blurred definition of the possible forms of mutual assistance and the territorial restrictions on the Alliance defense-area laid down in Article 5 were necessary preconditions for the isolationist influenced U.S. Congress of that time to ratify the North Atlantic Treaty and overcoming fears of entanglement, mainly "to see the US dragged automatically into yet another intra-European war".[43]

First and foremost, Article 5 constitutes the legal fiction that an attack against one NATO member immediately is an attack against all. All NATO member nations, therefore, are in this case obliged to support the attacked on the basis of their right to individual and collective self-defense according to Article 51 of the UN Charter. A compulsion to do this by *military* means or *collectively* does yet not exist. The letters of Article 5 leave open a wide possibility of defense activities, stipulating no more than that each NATO state "will assist the Party or Parties ... attacked by taking forthwith, individually and in concert with the other Parties, such action as it deems necessary, including the use of armed force, to restore and maintain the security of the North Atlantic area." Moreover, according to the last paragraph of Article 5, "[a]ny such armed attack and all measures taken as a result thereof shall immediately be reported to the [UN] Security Council. Such measures shall be terminated when the Security Council has taken the measures necessary to restore and maintain international peace and security."

All this should make it clear enough that, quite different from some contemporary allegations and hopes, NATO does not, and could not ever, aim to become a system of collective security. In its military component, NATO originally was designed as a mere *defense treaty* fulfilling rapid reaction functions until the UN Security Council would have initiated some appropriate measures on the basis of the UN's envisaged, yet never realized, system of global collective security. NATO would not be in a position to substitute for this unborn UN security system because it legally lacks some indispensable prerequisites for collective security. These are an automatism for force deployment and each member's unconditional obligation to take military action if necessary. Moreover, the Atlantic Alliance, like every defensive alliance, does not dispose of effective mechanisms for the case that the aggressor comes from within, as in the case of the Cyprus conflict between Greece and Turkey.

The 'old' NATO was well advised never to attempt to autonomously conduct UN operations, by way of substituting for the UN's vast operational inertia in security affairs. However, after its strategy revision in Rome of November 1991, it temporarily tended to slip precisely into that direction. In April 1993 and for the first time since its existence, it adopted a combat task, enforcing the no-fly zone over Bosnia, the success of which however, as some analysts of the U.S. Army War College's Strategic Studies Institute observed, concealed a pressing vital problem of its future: stopping the "'free fall' in its members national force structures".[44] The adaptation of the Alliance's command and control structures according to changed national capabilities and interests as well as the development of and agreement upon a blueprint for operational structures meeting foreseeable sub-strategic military needs (what then became the CJTF concept) did one not witness until the Berlin Ministerial Meeting of June 1996.

Strictly, NATO support missions for the UN cannot be derived from the North Atlantic Treaty. They remain paradoxical insofar as Article 5 demands that any operational NATO activity cease as soon as the UN Security Council has decided upon appropriate collective measures. On the other hand, this does not at all imply an argument against Alliance out-of-area engagement. Whereas one cannot honestly read any collective-security commitment out of (or into) the North Atlantic Treaty, nothing can hinder a coalition among some of its signatory nations to use common Alliance assets for multinational military intervention regardless of *any* territorial limits. The often-cited alleged 'regional limitation' of Article 6 is of no relevance here. Article 6 but defines the Alliance territory to be *attacked* in order to make this attack virtually an attack against all NATO members in the sense of Article 5, opening the way to common reaction, including, yet *not* demanding or requiring the use of military force. It is also in this context that the infamous Tropic of Cancer comes in. It is mentioned in Article 6 not in order to draw a line beyond which no NATO action may take place but to define certain islands which in a given case may become territory to defend (and others that may not). This so often misinterpreted regulation tributes to post-World War II U.S. fears to become entangled in European colonial conflicts.[45]

Therefore, just as little as one can derive from the Treaty's Articles a general ban of out-of-area activities can one derive from it any general obligation to support actions of such type. That however was already the formula of compromise found at the 1982 NATO Summit in Bonn. Finally, "strictly speaking, out-of-area events fall within the national competence of those allied governments which happen or wish to be involved."[46] Thus, the long and vociferous out-of-area discussions of the early 1990s were somewhat futile in large parts. And the practical outlook of a new, post-Cold War UN collective-security enthusiasm, with the world-organization backed by NATO assets or even 'commanding' NATO military operations was bleak from its beginning. In addition, as noted above, MC 327 alone and early enough shattered the dreams of adherents to the vision of a NATO-based system of collective security in Europe.

Indeed, many of the changes in NATO's defense concept and operational capabilities reflect not so much concrete threat perceptions or considerations of out-of-area action as they follow genuinely *political* requirements. The Allied Command Europe Rapid Reaction Corps (ARRC) and the concept of Combined Joint Task Forces (CJTF) not only fulfill operational but also important *political* functions. They exemplify the trend to secure Alliance cohesion in contingencies after the dissolution of the layer-cake principle. This principle consisted in writing Alliance solidarity literally into the landscape, namely by dividing the inner-German defense-line into several smaller defense sectors, each of which to be military defended by a different member state than the neighboring. Due to the small geographical extent of each of these sectors, a Warsaw Pact attack would have hit several NATO states at one time.

Not only in this sense are ARRC and CJTF rather indications of increased regional 'stickiness' of the Alliance than they point to envisaged routine out-of-area engagement. Also present shortcomings in transportation, especially airlift capacity suggest such an interpretation. They are for the most part legacies from the former shield-concept of territorial defense in the West European theater, the crucial point of which was not conventional force mobility but in contrast ability to hold one's assigned defense sector, thus blocking any advance of the Warsaw Pact troops.[47] During the Gulf War of 1991 for example, the dislocation of a German missile-defense system to southeastern Turkey posed a hard transportation problem for NATO. Finally, it could only be accomplished with the support of the Soviets, who after some back and forth put a large-capacity aircraft at disposal.

5. Global Factors Shaping the European Security Problématique

To sum up, it is indispensable to appreciate the global context, or paradoxically speaking the *global* dimension of *regional* security and security politics in Europe before turning to analyzing the Euro-regional system itself. In the course of this, important core conditions for an appropriate examination of NATO's adaptation and outlook can be clarified. The following points deserve special notice:

(1) Of the competing interpretations about the end of the Cold War and related expectations about the future, the (neo)realist point of view has proven to be adequate, at least as concerns security politics and the future of its institutional structures, as well as the (re)crescent relevance of national interests and emerging new forms of the security dilemma.

(2) Assuming an increasing (Euro-)regional relevance of the UN and its specific mechanisms for managing conflict is as unrealistic as expecting a globalization of NATO. Not only national interests run counter but also missing resources and military capabilities, such as - in the case of NATO - short-term deployability and long-distance projection.

(3) According to the proposed institutionalist methodology, it can be concluded that already the global constitutive context of the Euro-regional security problématique brings about a high degree in path-dependency, discontinuity and multicausality. Ideally, institutional change should naturally follow, if not anticipate, political problems and trends. Nevertheless, a continuous adaptation is improbable, and often enough it appears as if the problems and developments rather follow the institutions. An example is the case of ex-Yugoslavia, where the conflicts went through virtually all institutional steps: from individualist approaches such as mediatory groups and plans (for example the London Contact Group and the Vance-Owen Draft) over the UN peace-keeping debacle of the UNPROFOR mission, reprisals taken under co-operation of WEU, OSCE and NATO (for example the control of shipping in the Adriatic and on the Danube in order to enforce the embargo against Serbia and Montenegro) to the conference approach of Dayton and the UN-NATO co-action in order to implement it (that is, the IFOR and SFOR mission).

(4) Relating to the foregoing point, seemingly so concrete security cooperation, in the post-strategic security realm, is not only about military operativeness and crisis responsiveness but also about politics. Military arrangements have an important political meaning and in part even foremost fulfill political, rather than military-operational functions. Conversely, politically motivated cooperation programs can adopt, and form the core of, military operativeness (such as the PfP program, which largely contributed to set up the channels of command and control for the IFOR and SFOR missions, conducted by NATO and non-NATO nations together).

Finally, this section intended to clarify the overall effects of the global context of Euro-regional security acting as some important determinants of NATO's adaptation and roles. At the same time, the overview of the different interpretations of the meaning of the changed world-political setting after the Cold War and the derived alleged consequences for NATO clearly showed the difficulty determining the future of the Alliance and recommendable policy strategies just by recurring to models of global trends and 'pressure'. Here, useful as it has proven in the preceding part of the analysis, a clear caveat against neorealism's still predominant structural bias is in order.

Chapter Four
The Regional Dimension - NATO's Institutional Adaptation

1. NATO's Institutional Potential and Adaptation: A Multi-Level Process

Now that the global-international context of NATO's future has been explicated, analysis can proceed to the immediate context of the Alliance's institutional adaptation, that is, the Euro-regional setting. At first, it is in order to emphasize that making the case for an institutional analysis means everything but proclaiming a grand strategy of institution building as a program for future European security politics as well as the future of the Atlantic Alliance. In contrast, such a collective approach was at best possible under the conditions of the Cold War's bipolar structural overlay. During that period, in retrospective at least, single security issues were surprisingly easy to couple and de-couple, and the corresponding institutional designs were also well to sustain over crisis periods and changed initial conditions. Well-defined paths of communication existed, almost all of them equally relevant and interdependent, but if necessary easily enough to divide into their specific contents. That became possible in consequence of the evolution of sufficiently *issue-specific* disarmament and negotiation regimes, such as SALT I (Strategic Arms Limitation Talks), MBFR (Mutual Balanced Forces Reduction), CSCE, SALT II, respectively INF/START (Intermediate Range Nuclear Forces/Strategic Arms Reductions Talks), or the Stockholm process of confidence- and security-building measures.

Despite an unmistakable interdependence of those issues and common global context (East-Western relations), the different institutionalized forms of contact revealed some remarkable autonomy. Therefore, setbacks in one area could not immediately spread to another. Particularly because of the loose coupling, continuity in West-East-relations could also be maintained over periods of crisis. So for example after the break-off of the disarmament talks at Geneva in late 1983, the Stockholm conference on confidence-building and disarmament, started in January 1984, could serve as an alternative forum. This switch-over was made considerably easier by the fact that up to this point, important principles, norms, rules and procedures[1] had emerged between the super-powers as well as both blocs as such. Given the question of common security as an overarching common reference point in the light of the atomic overkill, procedures and contents could be transferred from one issue-area to another without great difficulty.

Such an *evolutionary* model as it would be typical of *neoliberal* thought in particular is nevertheless of no promise for the *new* Europe (whereas it seemingly continues to form at least the implicit basis of many contemporary security concepts, or rather philosophies, such as the one of 'interlocking institutions'). Its two decisive prerequisites were, namely, a common general political (and strategic) reference and at the same time a sufficiently clear specific content of each problem area. Especially the common reference is obviously missing today. It is true that it is on all sides about coming to terms with the requirements of diffuse 'new challenges'. Yet just these challenges are not collectively defined any more, but each single actor (from national governments and defense ministries up to international organizations like NATO or the UN) undertakes attempts to define the situation autonomously. Here, historical path-dependency comes in. Britain's post-Cold War defense Whitebooks for example are still oriented to the vision of global military engagement and force projection capabilities,[2] whereas the German Whitebook of 1994, owing to the tradition of 'Genscherism', in large parts still understands security policy as a kind of global peace-service for humankind[3]. Also the second prerequisite for successful institutional interlocking as it could be seen in the 1970ies and 80ies is hardly given today: There can be no question of specific, reciprocally separable contents and issues in the current institutional forms of European security politics (from NATO with NACC/EAPC and PfP over WEU and OSCE to the ESDI-project). Rather, the problems have become crosscutting and overlapping. Virtually all institutional forms of European security cooperation have adopted a strong all-regional, common-security component, and all claim responsibility for, or at least in principle envisage, a whole variety of forms of engagement, from humanitarian action and ethno-nationalist conflict management to international military operations.

In this atmosphere of institutional concurrence, the Atlantic Alliance's political goal-setting, in the political and military-operational area alike, has proven flexible enough to secure the maintenance of its integration until far beyond the turning point of 1989-90. What appears to be the critical point for NATO's future is less saving its mere existence as such or amending it by the adoption of new members than the question of its prospective *character* as a Euro-Atlantic security *institution* with the related informal rules, expectations, common interests, routinized political and military-operational procedures and a world-public image.[4] This suggests the proposition that sharply defined common (military) threat fading, *alliances* tend to show the appearance and problems typical of a security *community*.[5] Then the question of *internal*, mainly genuinely *political* mechanisms for both continued intra-Alliance cooperation and external effectiveness becomes decisive.[6]

Nevertheless, such a point of view is no methodological patent remedy either. For example, the currently so popular thesis that international institutions condition national adaptive behavior and the shape of common interests[7] tempts one - as argued above - to overlook the question how these *institutions* themselves adapt to changed international-political conditions, or if they are capable of such an adaptation anyway[8]. In this context, it can be shown that the ease of the bipolar overlay exposed NATO to classical international-political adaptive pressure in the structural-realist, Waltzian sense, meaning that changes in the international-political "structure" "shove" NATO as such towards certain courses of action so to maintain its 'position' in the international system.[9] This adaptive pressure firstly resulted from the 'trivial' necessity for military re-orientation after the strategic enemy's disappearance and growing national interests in cutting defense expenditures down, secondly of course from the emerging much-invoked 'new security tasks' (cf. for example the out-of-area debate) and finally from the fact that NATO, because of the political-military double function it has possessed from its foundation, was on the verge of drifting towards a sort of "self-proclaimed collective security organization", together with the according political principles and behavioral norms.[10] Yet in the end, structural realism à la Waltz finally does not seem quite applicable to that phenomenon. Its "units" are states, making international organizations and institutional forms fall out of its analytical scope. Despite, a structural-realist based model for NATO's institutional adaptation since 1990 is quite elucidating.

According to such a model of adaptive pressure, already NATO's "London Declaration" of July 1990 stated that "this Alliance must and will adapt."[11] The approach was, whereas retaining the primacy of collective self-defense, to sincerely review and revise the formulation of this common defense, so that

> the Alliance's integrated force structure and its strategy will change fundamentally to include the following elements:
>
> - NATO will field smaller and restructured active forces. These forces will be highly mobile and versatile so that Allied leaders will have maximum flexibility in deciding how to respond to a crisis. It will rely increasingly on multinational corps made up of national units.
> - NATO will scale back the readiness for its active units, reducing training requirements and the number of exercises.
> - NATO will rely more heavily on the ability to build up larger forces if and when they might be needed.[12]

This identified imperative of adaptation found its concrete political and military consequence in "The Alliance's new Strategic Concept" as agreed upon during the Rome Summit of November 1991. Accordingly (amending, not replacing, its traditional political and military functions), three new roles for NATO were envisaged: the "dialogue with other nations", an "active search for a cooperative approach to European security" and complementing as well as reinforcing "political actions within a broad approach to security", thereby contributing with the "Alliance's military forces" to the "management of such crises and their peaceful resolution" that "might lead to a military threat to the security of Alliance members".[13] One further component of this plan for institutional adaptation was to establish a concrete "diplomatic liaison"[14] with the former Warsaw Pact countries, which subsequently found its institutional formation in the set-up of the North Atlantic Cooperation Council in December 1991 and the Partnership for Peace program in January 1994.

With the end of the Cold War and the collapse of the Warsaw Pact, NATO moreover consciously turned to a 'generalized' enemy. Correspondingly, the new Strategic Concept stated:

> In contrast with the predominant threat of the past, the risks to Allied security that remain are multi-faceted in nature and multi-directional, which makes them hard to predict and assess. NATO must be capable of responding to such risks if stability in Europe and the security of Alliance members are to be preserved. These risks can arise in various ways.[15]

That way, the Strategic Concept precisely did not give up the traditional core functions of the Alliance but reaffirmed them - at the same time acknowledging the need for far-reaching institutional changes exactly because of the continuance of its principle rationale.

Here one particular paradox in NATO's institutional adaptation to the post-Cold War setting becomes obvious, which makes it clear that any meaningfully institutional perspective on contemporary Euro-Atlantic security must at least *combine* neorealist and neoliberal assumptions, instead of trying to play them off against each other. The paradox could be termed the *structural-functional paradox* and has shown up in NATO's development since 1990. Neoliberalism predicted NATO's continued existence as such, yet if only in the pure sense of self-resistance against dissolution and with recourse to sweeping axioms like the alleged striving of states for low transaction costs in international cooperation.[16] What neoliberalism did not predict were *qualitative* institutional changes. Rather, according to its assumption of trivial institutional stickiness over changed settings and faded initial founding interests,[17] it had to expect a *functional* reorientation of NATO under retention of its structure - which Keohane explicitly predicted[18]. What NATO however showed by the end of its first wave of adaptation was, contrarily, a *structural reorientation under retention of its essential founding function* (that is providing for common defense and concentrating on military concerns). The Madrid Declaration of July 1997 became most explicit about this:

> NATO will remain the essential forum for consultation among its members and the venue for agreement on policies bearing on the security and defence commitments of Allies under the Washington Treaty. ... While maintaining our core function of collective defence, we have adapted our political and military structures to improve our ability to meet the new challenges of regional crisis and conflict management.[19]

This functional perseverance, as opposed to mere structural tenacity, had already loomed through as early as in December 1991, in the new Strategic Concept:

> Two conclusions can be drawn from this analysis of the strategic context. The first is that the new environment does not change the purpose or the security functions of the Alliance, but rather underlines their enduring validity. The second, on the other hand, is that the changed environment offers new opportunities for the Alliance to frame its strategy within a broad approach to security. ... NATO's essential purpose, set out in the Washington Treaty and reiterated in the London Declaration, is to safeguard the freedom and security of all its members by political and military means in accordance with the principles of the United Nations Charter. Based on common values of democracy, human rights and the rule of law, the Alliance has worked since its inception for the establishment of a just and lasting peaceful order in Europe. This Alliance objective remains unchanged.[20]

However, the new Strategic Concept had not marked much more than a fairly common agreement on NATO's future and the imminent necessities of organizational and operational change. One manifest statement was *that* it would be all about a fundamental, also organizational, adaptation to new political and military challenges while preserving the primacy of collective defense. Still, even this consensus was in large part a product of the member states' self-interest, some of which were seeking to ease their stretched defense budgets by creating new, collectively financed, multi-national force structures.[21]

Therefore, the Atlantic Alliance's unexpected capacity for adapting to changed conditions, at the same time preserving and extending its traditional legitimization, can - paradoxically - not be sufficiently explained by its *autonomous* functional potential. Well corresponding to the institutionalist axioms suggested above, such as discontinuity of change and multiple causation, a complementing recourse to explanatory factors on the level of NATO's constitutive actors (which are and remain its member states) is indispensable.[22] Such a perspective on the constitutive actors suggests that the Alliance's rapid common reaction to the emerging new challenges was not the 'evolutionary' result of enlightened, entwined or multilateralized interests of the majority of NATO states (as neoliberalism and normative theory could argue) but rather an example of the principle of the "self-reliant optimality potential" of international "bargaining solutions"[23].

Accordingly, the growth of international institutional forms is always co-determined by the will of the relevant states to let the related developments pass beyond their direct, unilateral influence. In international institutional settings, then, states typically lose abilities and opportunities to influence unilaterally the related outcomes or organizational behavior to the credit of politically leveled, "comprehensively efficient solutions".[24] At the same time however, they gain the chance of bringing in their own goals freely and (at least according to the fiction) without regard to their status or relative position - whereas avoiding exclusive responsibility for the consequences of the collective solutions found, although each single state can profit from effective solutions, regardless of its own contribution.[25]

Independently, this principle has recently been introduced in structural neorealist theorizing as "voice opportunity"-proposition, borrowing from organization theory.[26] Of distinguished interest here is "the level of policy influence partners have or might attain in the collaborative arrangement."[27] Following on from this, assumptions out of neorealist and organization theory - taken each themselves, as argued above, unsuited for adequately appreciating the process and determinants of NATO's adaptation - flow together into an institutionalist argument that underscores the importance of 'soft', contextual factors in rational state action and international cooperation. According to the voice-opportunity proposition, and against neoliberalism, states not only seek institutional arrangements to make cooperation cheaper and increase their individual substantive gains but also to find conductive contexts and opportunities to effectively articulate and circulate their national policies:

> [I]t points to the possibility that states may look at a collaborative arrangement in terms both of the substantive benefits and the *opportunities for effective voice it provides*. 'Effective voice opportunities' may be defined as institutional characteristics whereby the views of partners (including relatively weaker partners) are not just expressed but reliably have a material impact on the operations of the collaborative arrangement. ... In other words, states (and particularly weaker states) may view effective voice as a 'good' that they enjoy as part of being in a collaborative arrangement, and enjoyment of a satisfactory level of this 'good' may itself be a basis for assessment by states of their satisfaction or dissatisfaction with the arrangement.[28]

The voice-opportunity proposition offers a common denominator for a bunch of developments significant for the future of NATO and post-strategic security in Europe. It can, for example, well account for France's rapprochement to (but not reintegration into) the Alliance's military structure, assuming that the French government was seeking to broaden its available contexts for national policy and interest articulation in the light of NATO's increasing politicization after the end of bipolarity. Moreover, it can explain the success of NATO's initiatives for cooperation with its former adversaries, PfP and NACC, as well as some former Warsaw Pact countries' pressing wishes to become regular members of NATO and Russian demands for a security charter codifying its relation to the Alliance. All these developments may be interpreted as attempts to open up a well-practiced institutional context, that of the Atlantic

Alliance, for purposes of making oneself and one's national policies more visible on a European scale.

Nevertheless, a complete institutionalist analysis of NATO's adaptation has to delve still further into its constitutive context, looking into the dimension of *intergovernmental bargaining*. Intergovernmental bargaining can well account for the often not too well understood parallelism of different approaches to institutionalize post-strategic European or Euro-Atlantic security cooperation as well as for the existence of institutional fragments that seem not quite to fit into the current setting but despite endure and function. This again hints upon the path-dependency and multicausality of institutional development and once more suggests that there can be no one grand strategy of institutional design. Here is an instructive example concerning intergovernmental bargaining about the shape of the envisaged European pillar of the Atlantic Alliance:[29]

During the Bush Presidency, the United States were responding openly reserved to reviving European attempts to develop an own security and defense identity (and a related operative reactivation of the WEU). The "Bartholomew telegram", a sharp diplomatic note the U.S. government sent to WEU's then-Secretary General, Willem van Eekelen, harshly shattered the illusion that a harmonic co-action of NATO on the one hand and the WEU as well as a European Common Foreign and Security Policy on the other could be accomplished. In a letter to all then-EC member states' governments, then-Secretary of State James Baker repeated the objections expressed in the Bartholomew telegram less sharply and at the same time made the Bush administration's acknowledgment and support of the envisaged European Security and Defense Identity (ESDI) dependent on several criteria to be met by the Europeans: All related developments should, in the final analysis, strengthen the Atlantic Alliance's effectiveness and keep it the main forum for all questions of European security; NATO must be able to maintain and if possible even deepen its integrated military structure; to avoid conflicts between the Europeans over the concrete shape of ESDI which may also weaken the Alliance, all related considerations and steps should not be undertaken but by all European NATO members together.

These U.S. demands rendered for example Germany in a precarious position, actually coming close to forcing it to choose between the transatlantic security link and its traditional security bilateralism with France. To this pressure for decision added the fact that at NATO's Ministerial Meeting in Copenhagen in June 1991, the U.S. had succeeded to thwart French plans for a rapid reaction force within the WEU in favor of a British lead NATO-troop, which then became the Allied Command Europe Rapid Reaction Corps (ARRC). In a remarkable diplomatic move, German Chancellor Helmut Kohl managed to escape the imposed decisional pressure through a package solution. In the "October initiative", together with the French President François

Mitterand, he announced a plan to incorporate the development of ESDI into the creation of the European Union by making the WEU into the then future European Union's defense component. The first step, the initiative proposed, should be made by a combined Franco-German corps, which in the meantime has become the Eurocorps. The almost parallel creation and existence of the Eurocorps and the ARRC thus is a conspicuous expression of the just described Euro-American and more specifically Franco-German-American interest conflict over the further institutionalization of a European security identity and package strategy applied by the Kohl-Mitterand chief-of-government, or "COG", collusion[30] in order to defuse it.

This relevance of bargaining factors at first sight seems a strong argument in favor of neoliberalism, but a closer look makes it clear that neoliberal connotations of bargaining are too narrow-focused here. Typically, as noted earlier, for neoliberalism bargaining entails intentionally establishing common 'institutional' constraints so to stabilize cooperation and overcoming the political market failure, that is sub-optimal outcomes of cooperative arrangements where Pareto-optimal, 'perfect' outcomes would have been reachable as well. Once established, those 'institutional' forms of international cooperation, in turn, are supposed to exert an enlightening effect on the national interests of the states involved. Apart from the fact that considerations of such kind hardly deserve being called in a proper sense 'institutionalist' (for they do not really allow to conceive of institutions themselves, *their* change and sustainability as distinct from the interests of and cooperative phenomena between their constitutive actors), they cannot account for *discontinuous* institutional developments. That is because the market-failure axiom and others may answer the general 'how?' yet certainly do not answer the concrete 'why and when?' of cooperation. Also have they little to say about interdependence between 'actors' and institutional 'structures' and about how much and how strong structural opportunities actors need to act effectively or, conversely, to what degree positive structural effects on cooperative behavior are dependent on benign actors, or 'agents'.[31]

To accomplish a complete 'how' *and* 'why' explanation, as proponents of the social theory of international relations, with Alexander Wendt first, have pointed out, it is therefore necessary to link "'structural' analysis", which typically "explains the possible" (for instance the common interactional context with its affordances and constraints), with a more "'historical' analysis" that allows for the delimitation of the "actual" within the structurally explained general institutional context.[32] This "historical", or "actual", analysis is concerned with individual actors and action strategies, as opposed to the materialized institutional framework structural analysis primarily looks at. Both however cannot be sensibly conducted, or even be conceived of, as separate analytical steps delving into distinct phenomena. In contrast, as Wendt further has emphasized, "agents are inseparable from social structures in the sense that their action is possible only in virtue of those structures, and social structures cannot have causal significance except insofar as they are enacted by agents. Social action, then, is co-determined by the properties of both agents and social structures."[33]

This assertion of a *continuous reciprocal co-determinism* between the agents constituting an institutional form and the shape and development of that institutional form itself well corresponds to the assumptions within the neoinstitutionalist paradigm in general social science.[34] As far as NATO's adaptation and strategy definition after 1990 is concerned, this methodological background of any sound institutionalist analysis makes at least two things clear. Firstly, the impact of bargaining is a necessary amendment of, not a contradiction to institutionally focused analysis; secondly, that delimitation is again to be amended by a focus upon actual actions of actual actors in actual situations (Wendt's "historical" dimension) and their cognitive foundations still beyond the scope of the international bargaining approach.

Thus, in addition to the mentioned state strategies of self-interest calculation and bargaining, creative acts of individual actors are to be taken into consideration so to arrive at complete explanations of the course and content of NATO's approach to the post-strategic condition. For example, the Alliance's general strategy revision was temporarily interrupted by derivative attempt to secure NATO's continued relevance and public support by way of ad hoc-activism. An illustrating example is the Venice speech of May 1993, delivered by then-Secretary General Manfred Wörner, in which he proclaimed a tactic of selective shop-window operations. He was much inspired by the assumption that NATO was in acute danger of losing its obvious "raison d'être", notably in the perception of its member states' electorates, and thus forced to present itself to the world public as an indispensable provider of "security and stability"[35]. For that sake, Wörner stressed, it should not make available its capabilities to the UN but self-responsibly engage in such conflicts that promise to be well-suited for making the Alliance's genuine "usefulness in dealing with immediate crises and problems"[36]. Consequently, Wörner cautioned, NATO would have to strictly refrain from any intervention in conflicts and crises where not publicly visible success could be expected or where NATO could not lead the related operations independently, especially in terms of military command and control.[37]

Underscoring NATO's further right to exist and its military operability in the face of post-strategic security threats was an important but only the one side of the coin. There remained another challenge: to elaborate a clear concept for the intended future military and political forms of defense cooperation and integration, reflecting the post-strategic security condition on a long-term basis.[38]

2. From 'Interlocking' over 'Interblocking' to 'Interacting'

This second side of the coin was soon realized, and the Brussels Summit of January 1994 marked a turn to the questions of concrete structural adaptation. The CJTF concept laid the basis for NATO's military-operative readjustment (the definitive design of which however was not agreed upon before the Berlin Ministerial Meeting of June 1996), and the PfP program with its bilateral cooperative arrangements took to solving the question of a well-defined political and strategic outreach to Central and Eastern Europe, beyond the diffuse idea of a general transfer of stability from West to East.[39]

So the Summit of Brussels brought a significant step towards revising the concept of the Alliance's institutional adaptation from an at first seemingly envisaged catch-all approach to a more promising strategy of functional restraint:

> 7. In pursuit of our common transatlantic security requirements, NATO increasingly will be called upon to undertake missions in addition to the traditional and fundamental task of collective defence of its members, which remains a core function. We reaffirm our offer to support, on a case by case basis in accordance with our own procedures, peacekeeping and other operations under the authority of the UN Security Council or the responsibility of the CSCE, including by making available Alliance resources with expertise. Participation in any such operation or mission will remain subject to decisions of member states in accordance with national constitutions.
>
> 8. Against this background, NATO must continue the adaptation of its command and force structure in line with requirements for flexible and timely responses contained in the Alliance's Strategic Concept. We also need to strengthen the European pillar of the Alliance by facilitating the use of our military capabilities for NATO and European/WEU operations, and assist participation of non-NATO partners in joint peacekeeping and other contingencies as envisaged under the Partnership for Peace.
>
> 9. Therefore, we direct the North Atlantic Council in Permanent Session, with the advice of the NATO Military Authorities, to examine how the Alliance's political and military structures and procedures might be developed and adapted to conduct more efficiently and flexibly the Alliance's missions. Including peacekeeping, as well as to improve cooperation with the WEU and to reflect the emerging European Security and Defence Identity. As part of this process, we endorse the concept of Combined Joint Task Forces as a means to facilitate contingency operations, including operations with participating nations outside the Alliance. We have directed the North Atlantic Council, with the advice of the NATO Military Authorities, to develop this concept and establish the necessary capabilities. The Council, with the advice of the NATO Military Authorities, and in coordination with the WEU, will work on implementation in a manner that provides separable but not separate military capabilities that could be employed by NATO or the WEU.[40]

Important to notice, much of NATO's adaptive endeavors are, despite its grown institutional autonomy, still best accountable to national interest-calculations. Even the decision taken back in November 1991 to establish the North Atlantic Cooperation Council (NACC) as an instrument to defuse the immediate pressure to decide about the when, how and who of an eastward expansion cannot sufficiently be explained as a deliberate policy of institution-building but has also to be seen in the classical realist sense, that is, in the light of national interests. In retrospect, NACC especially furthered two basic German interests: establishing an institutional framework fostering compliance with the disarmament regulations of the Treaty about Conventional Forces in Europe (CFE) and providing for continued international safeguard of the reunification's consequences in the field of European security (for example the subsequent expansion of NATO's military structures and area of defense to the territory of the former German Democratic Republic).[41]

France however took this as attempts to set up a German-U.S. bilateralism in security affairs, and anticipating political isolation, it replied with a counter-balancing strategy in the form of institutional duplication. That way it sought to decrease the relative importance of NATO and its new institutional ramifications, such as NACC. This counter-balancing was realized through the WEU, which at a French proposal was supplemented by a consultative forum consisting of selected Central and East European countries.[42] Notably, the French behavior was in perfect accordance with the power-principle of classical realism and the structural logic of Waltzian neorealism - both nowadays so often sweepingly reprimanded as obsolete.

Whereas NATO's initial post-Cold War strategic impetus, that was functionally confining itself to military tasks, especially collective self-defense, quickly became visibly blurred in the course of the out-of-area debate and subsequently in the enlargement discussion, a strategy of self-limitation would now as before be appropriate and advisable - for the Atlantic Alliance remains an indispensable and effective, but is not any longer a *comprehensive* 'security provider'. When in November 1991 the North Atlantic Council came up with the formula of "interlocking institutions"[43], it obviously believed the Alliance to be able to play a general leading role in devising future European security structures and accordingly, it declared: "The Alliance is the essential forum for consultation among its members and the venue for agreement on policies bearing on the security and defence commitments of Allies under the Washington Treaty."[44]

This vision however soon found itself disappointed, when other European security institutions promulgated their own, competing concepts for the future. The first step made the newly founded European Union as soon as in February 1992, with its Common Foreign and Security Policy (CFSP) and the project of a common European Security and Defense Identity (ESDI), followed by the WEU with its Petersberg Declaration and the Conference on Security and Cooperation in Europe (CSCE), which - symbol enough - assembled in Helsinki, its founding location, and presented a comprehensive program for future European security. To a large part, the history of European security politics after 1989-90 can indeed be written as a history of "institutional rivalry".[45]

Given this institutional competition, it is problematic that after the end of bipolarity, NATO - while *militarily* sticking to collective defense - *politically* has repeatedly striven for a general involvement in the European broad political agenda, which it early institutionalized in the form of NACC and the subsequent EAPC. This contributed to the concept of *interlocking institutions* under political and strategic guidance of the Atlantic Alliance threatening to become in practice rather a functionally unspecified, more inhibiting than reinforcing juxtaposition of *interblocking institutions*. NATO's attempt to present itself as the leading 'stability-projector' early enough adopted paradoxical forms.[46] For example, the Alliance not only collectively admitted the Soviet successor states into NACC - despite of the involvement of three of them either in war-type conflicts with one another (Armenia and Azerbaijan) or with secessionist groups (Georgia). The member states of NATO also, while facing growing problems with their attempts to settle the war in their immediate strategic neighborhood (ex-Yugoslavia), successively broadened the Alliance's self-declared security guaranteeship: In June 1992 CSCE was officially offered operational support, reaching up to NATO conducting peace-keeping operations under a CSCE mandate, and in December the UN Security Council was offered a similar kind of support.

Here once again the Berlin Ministerial Meeting of June 1996 marked a decisive turning point: Whereas the Defense Committee and the Nuclear Planning Group had still maintained in its meeting in November 1995 that "[t]he Alliance continues to be the linchpin of European security"[47], half a year later in Berlin NATO gave up its claim to a leading role in the interplay of European security institutions, thus relinquishing the organizing principle of *interlocking institutions* and turning to a new principle that could be termed the one of *interacting institutions* - namely a coordinated interplay of the different post-strategic security strategies and institutions in Europe that does not rest upon one lead-institution but rather on the idea of general common regulations for a well-defined functional sharing of burden, commitment and responsibility. Nonetheless, the different institutions, according to this idea, will not be isolated from one another but interconnected especially by using common organizational assets.

That became conspicuous in the North Atlantic Council practically charging the West Europeans, respectively the WEU, to develop an own military operativeness,[48] which effectively meant to establish the since the times of De

Gaulle so much debated European pillar *within* NATO itself. This pillar however is not to set up a European parallel structure to the traditional transatlantic pillar, but in contrast to be "separable but not separate" from it.[49] This is to be ensured by two structural interconnections: on the one hand the concept of Allied Combined Joint Task Forces (CJTF), that is, integrated operational command and control nuclei attached to selected sub-strategic NATO commands but at the same time, as the case may be, removable from NATO's command and control structure and available for Europeans-only operations, for example within the WEU framework; on the other hand the principle of *double hatting*, that is, making forces answerable both to NATO and WEU.

The CJTF-concept, more precisely, refers to building military headquarter cells with some steady command and staff elements but no permanent military integration, let alone a standing rapid reaction force.[50] Its innovative element are permanent multinational-headquarter nuclei - in contrast to the up to now prevailing ad-hoc arrangements for the command and control structures of multinational military operations beyond collective self-defense. Structurally, CJTF rests upon a kind of double unit-construction system. According to the type of mission - firstly - among all nations wishing to participate in a certain action, force units optimized for the foreseeable tasks are identified and then - secondly - taken out of the respective national units, combined and assigned the CJTF Headquarter selected and augmented for the operation in question.

CJTF perfectly exemplifies the path-dependency of institutional innovation, its co-determination by past decisions and also the multiple causation of institutional change. Altogether, in addition to its strict military-operational functions, CJTF can fulfill a fivefold coordinating task.[51] First, it can guarantee, by developing clear-cut criteria, that multinational force units really become effectively integrated and operative. CJTF should help to counteract the tendency prevalent in some NATO countries to contribute to multinational units, yet mainly in order to ease one's *own* defense budget and consequently not ensuring that the respective forces are trained and equipped in a way that actually allows for multinational interoperability. Second, CJTF can provide a common framework for joint exercises of NATO and PfP nations' military forces, helping to smooth the way to enduring cooperation in military and security affairs. Third, CJTF allows for linking NATO countries not (yet) integrated into the Alliance's military structure (as it is currently the case for France and Spain, naturally as well as the prospective new members) to that structure. Fourth, CFTF Headquarters may serve as coordinating agencies between NATO and WEU or a future European defense organization in the framework of the forming European Security and Defense Identity. Moreover, the CJTF Headquarters have the strategic function of providing WEU on a case-by-case basis with the necessary military and command-and-control infrastructure for own operations. Fifth, also as a political function, CJTF Headquarters could act as connection authorities to the UN. That way, a strong coordinating cord, also defining clear political and operational responsibilities, could be established for NATO-missions conducted in implementation of Security Council resolutions.

In the final analysis, by the Ministerial Meeting in Berlin in June 1996 and with the decisions taken there, NATO seemed in large parts to have returned to where it had been on the point of turning to in 1989, just before the political upheavals in the Eastern bloc ushered in its search for a new strategic concept, position in the network of European security institutions and general political rationale. In a hardly noticed study of 1989, a special committee set up by the North Atlantic Assembly presented a report on "NATO in the 1990s"[52]. Far from having been out-dated by the subsequent events, reading it today could make one think that it was projected somewhere in early 1996, in the face of the Berlin Ministerial Meeting.

Among some of the remarkable conclusions were the assumption of an increased French rapprochement to NATO's military structures,[53] the call for increased European cooperation within the Alliance, possibly using the WEU as an operational basis,[54] and the recommendation of increased military task-specialization[55]. Especially the then-conception of task specialization could be instructive for the ongoing CJTF-implementation process, which typically focuses on the collectivity aspect of the concept ("coalitions of the willing") rather than the specialization aspect. The specialization aspect (not all necessary or desirable CJTF-modules can, and should be, provided for by all member states) however should not be so neglected. Especially with a view to the military-operational aspects of enlargement, it could provide some important clues for determining both specific possible contributions and standardization need for the prospective members - thus completing the question of *general interoperability* (or, what a prospective member has to do to meet operational NATO requirements) by that of specific *functional capabilities* of each country (or, what a prospective member has to offer to specifically contribute to NATO's needs in the new era of post-strategic security). As the 1989 report, when nobody would have anticipated considerably shrinking national defense budgets or even dreamt of a NATO enlargement and new smaller allies joining the Alliance, aptly proposed,

> the European allies should seek to encourage task specialization among themselves as a way of eliminating wasteful duplication and overlap among national military efforts. There are substantial barriers to specialization deeply rooted in military history and contemporary political and economic priorities of member nations. But the limited resource base for sustaining necessary defense improvements would appear increasingly to demand that smaller allies in particular take on special tasks well suited to their geographic location and na-

tional resources as part of a tasking strategy organized on a European level and compatible with NATO planning requirements.[56]

Increasing the chances of those recommendations to become reality as well as confirming the observed trends towards an approach of *interacting* institutions, the Ministerial Meeting at Sintra in May 1997 marked a further step to the Alliance explicitly acknowledging the multilateralized character of poststrategic European security. As for the relationship between NATO and WEU, for example, the Final Communiqué stated:

> We welcome agreement reached recently in the WEU on the participation of all European Allies, if they were so to choose, in WEU operations using NATO assets and capabilities, as well as in planning and preparing of such operations; and on involvement, to the fullest extent possible and in accordance with their status, of Observers in the follow-up, within the WEU, of our meetings of Berlin and Brussels. We note that the basis has therefore been established for the implementation of Ministerial decisions, for the strengthening of NATO-WEU working relations and, in this framework, for the development of the ESDI with the full participation of all European Allies. This will ... contribute to setting the groundwork for possible WEU-led operations with the support of Alliance assets and capabilities.[57]

3. The Mixed Menu of European Security - NATO Enlargement as an Example

Whereas the example of NATO's internal adaptation shows the elucidating contributions of institutionalist *methodology* (such as path-dependency, discontinuity and multiple causation), the specific issue-area of NATO expansion poses ponderous *theoretical* questions. Briefly, from a theoretical point of view, NATO enlargement is still quite a paradox, even after being formally decided. Judging by common theoretical perspectives, it should never have come up - a fact that even Hellmann's and Wolf's seminal analysis[58] of alternative theoretical predictions about NATO's future overlooked. None of our common grand theories is able to explain *why* at the Brussels Summit of January 1994, the Alliance members set the - albeit rather vague - sign of a coming expansion[59] and then remarkably strictly followed a corresponding political course.

Structural realism, for example, would absolutely have acknowledged that international-political adaptive pressure as arising from the collapse of the Warsaw Pact and some Russian neo-imperialist tendencies may "shove"[60] Central and Eastern European states towards NATO. Waltz deems national self-renunciation of such kind abnormal in a sense but concedes it possible if pursued for precisely the sake of a unit's own survival.[61] Alternatively, this trend could always be explained in terms of bandwagoning:[62] In order to secure their newly reached positions as sovereign powers, the members of the 'losing' Alliance choose to figuratively jump on the train of the winning coalition. Alas, the whole enlargement discussion per se, from a neorealist point of view, was perfectly at odds with the standard assumption of an immanent decline of alliances after the loss of their immediate adversary. Waltz and Mearsheimer had prominently predicted such an immanent and inevitable decline of NATO.[63]

Neoliberalism, on the other side, could always have put NATO's continued existence as well as its enlargement down to the fact that institutional forms are (for some important part at least) independent forces in world politics, which - if only somehow functional - tend to preserve themselves or even to widespread. Yet it cannot explain why any state should ever develop an interest in increasing the number of Alliance members. That is because neoliberalism assumes that states will always prefer small cooperative arrangements - among other things because otherwise transaction costs would exceed the respective calculations of individual gain.[64] This surely also applies to the anticipated costs of national adaptation to a broad revision of current common Alliance positions and bargaining about new political and defense tasks and commitments - all necessities in the course of enlargement. Accordingly, Keohane himself once declared *institutional closure* to be one of the cornerstones of neoliberal assumptions.[65]

As for the question of NATO's and its member states' adaptation to a new membership structure, it again becomes obvious that taking the historicity (or path-dependency) and multicausality of institutional development seriously forecloses any hopes of rational *grand design*-type solutions. Increased Alliance membership will strongly demand both strategic and institutional reforms - already so not to risk to minimize its ability of collective decision-making. Moreover, as has often been overlooked, the question of enlargement is not exclusively one of high NATO politics but also considerably concerns the smaller member states (as for example Spain or Portugal), which will be facing severe cuts in military support programs.[66]

An enlarged NATO of course will have to direct all its related capabilities eastward in order to establish there as soon as possible feasible military structures and lead the new members' defense policies and capabilities alike up to Western standards. Otherwise, the Atlantic Alliance would render itself hampered and consequentially obsolete exactly *by* embarking on a strategy of institutional adaptation, innovation and outreach. Additionally, as a consequence of expansion, currently comparatively well contained regional problems and conflict potentials on the post-Soviet territory could newly pose themselves as common Alliance problems in one go. NATO will unavoidably have to take up the question of how to handle conflicts between new members (whereas its historical record shows that it has not always performed well in defusing conflicts between its old members, just to mention Suez and Cyprus). Institutionalization and institutional adaptation should therefore not at all be equated with improved conflict transformation or even resolution, as do many proponents of neoliberalism -[67] for it might only trigger the escalation or amplification of conflicts as well as create new ones.

In well accordance with the classical realist national interest-doctrine, it has to be acknowledged that the question of NATO expansion is anything but an end in itself or the logical consequence of any self-generating tendency of institutional evolution. Rather, single national decision-makers handled it in ways that promised best compliance with their respective interests. Great Britain for example had never been especially interested in fast enlargement, precisely due to its strongly NATO-oriented defense and security policy. The anticipated temporary weakening of the Alliance was suspected to considerably reduce Britain's say in international security affairs. It is different with the case of Germany, which is characterized by a relatively small say in Alliance security matters - due to its nuclear poverty and traditional multilateralism in security affairs. Accordingly, Germany now and again tried to present itself as an advocate of some of the newly independent states' desire for economy and security integration. France's position had over long periods been characterized by the fear of, having left NATO's military integration in 1966, becoming politically isolated in the course of enlargement. The U.S. were suspected to pull the wires, trying to secure themselves a strong political stance in the new Europe at French expense.

The NATO-enlargement puzzle highlights an important shortcoming in current International Relations modeling and theorizing as outlined in the introduction: There is no international *institutional* theory that could allow for treating international organizations in their institutional peculiarity, which however is limited by the continued relevance of national interest-type calculations as alluded to above, and thus not at the same time losing relation to the constitutive actors, their strategies and interests. Such a theory would have to be not structurally based but to recur to the idea of continued *securitization* according to the Copenhagen school as mentioned in the beginning. Security and security politics, then, should be understood as multi-level and multi-context problems, being on their best way to involve real *politics* and not merely questions of military strategy and narrow gain-calculations. The multiplicitly co-determined character of the emerging post-strategic security problems and politics should lead one to expect less concentrated, in the common sense 'institutionalized' configurations of actors, interests and political structures than continuous processes of de- and restructuring beyond or parallel to existing, organized forms of political order, such as the North Atlantic Treaty Organization.

If one seeks at the same time to highlight the fact that even under the conditions of a new *géométrie variable* in the wake of the emerging era of post-strategic security in Europe, there are relatively constant and enduring *configurations* of actors and political structures, which as a consequence of a common historical background, of specific crosscutting issues or simply of geostrategic vicinity exert effects of political standardization upon the actors, it will be most feasible to employ the concept of a "security complex"[68]. With a special view to the European situation since 1989, it emphasizes the genuinely *institutional* aspect of international security and security politics: its character as a process formation rather than a fixed state or strategy, and therefore comprising different scopes and reference points.

These of course repetitively find their expression in concrete situations and problem structures but themselves are subject to continuous redefinition - even if over time, typical actors, issues and interaction patterns will arise in each security complex. It follows therefrom that European security politics will not let itself be conceived of and conducted as defined by fixed coalitions of actors, structures of alliances and alignments, security institutions or normative models, but that it will have to be understood as essentially a process of continued securitization (or, as the case may be, de-securitization). Thus, one will have to expect flexible actor groupings, strategies and interests, changing depending on the situation or security concern in question.

Contrarily to prevalent policy metaphors in question of European security, not vacuum-absorbing projection of stability towards Central and Eastern Europe forms the decisive stake but founding general "behavioral regimes" in the "post-Soviet security space", reaching from minority protection to arms control and crisis management.[69] Many features of the prospect for institutional flexibility and fluidity of post-strategic European security have recently become obvious in the institutional reform of NATO. Here it is conspicuous that *security* has fully become *politics*. This trend was well exemplified by NATO's Berlin decision to set up a Policy Coordination Group (PCG). Increasingly important is not the common reaction to a clearly defined threat and challenge by means of a new grand strategy or - speaking in terms of structural realism - keeping one's position in the international game of power but the act of *positioning* oneself in new regional frameworks and general political settings.

Selective multi-state cooperation in changing coalitions will become both typical of and crucial for NATO's relevance and effectiveness. The plans devised at Berlin to implement the CJTF-concept directly into NATO's strategy and to adjust its command and headquarters structure to CJTF-like needs confirm this assumption. This requires on the side of the member states the willingness and ability to (re)define their relations to NATO and with one another from one issue to the next. Such a multilateralism will entail different coalitions within the Alliance, as the case may be, for example for conflict-intervention in implementation of UN resolutions, for humanitarian assistance or for purposes such as helping to stabilize the transitions in Central and Eastern Europe.

As regards the Alliance's concrete operational and political Eastern outreach, the clearest sign indicating a multilateralist approach as just outlined is the Euro-Atlantic Partnership Council (EAPC), established in May 1997, and its actions program. According to the EAPC Basic Document,

> [t]he Euro-Atlantic Partnership Council, as the successor to NACC, will provide the overarching framework for consultations among its members on a broad range of political and security-related issues, as part of a process that will develop through practice. PfP in its enhanced form will be a clearly identifiable element within this flexible framework. Its basic elements will remain valid. The Euro-Atlantic Partnership Council will build upon the existing framework of NATO's outreach activities preserving their advantages to promote cooperation in a transparent way. The expanded political dimension of consultation and cooperation which the Council will offer will allow Partners, if they wish, to develop a direct political relationship individually or in smaller groups with the Alliance. In addition, the Council will provide the framework to afford Partner countries, to the maximum extent possible, increased decision-making opportunities relating to activities in which they participate.
>
> ... The Euro-Atlantic Partnership Council will retain two important principles which have underpinned the success of cooperation between Allies and Partners so far. It will be inclusive, in that opportunities for political consultation and practical cooperation will be open to all Allies and Partners equally. It will also maintain self-differentiation, in that Partners will be able to decide for themselves the level and areas of cooperation with NATO. Arrangements under the Council will not affect commitments already undertaken bilaterally between Partners and NATO, or commitments in the PfP Framework Document.[70]

Chapter Five
The National Dimension - Individual vs. Common Goods

1. Internal Linkages of Post-strategic Security Cooperation

However much the Atlantic Alliance deserves it, as explained above, to be conceived of as an increasingly self-reliant, remarkable stable institution with important corporate traits beyond narrow reflection of its member states' national interest calculations, it is precisely that *national context* that any sound scholarly analysis and political conception alike must not miss to decently appraise. After all, the 'new' NATO remains an *inter*national, as opposed to a supranational institution. And when, in the context of the newly emerging security challenges and the question of appropriate international institutions, disseminating the idea of a "multipolar peace", "constitutional foundations of world peace" or even a "post-modern" or post-strategic politics of peace,[1] one should consequently focus upon those 'sub-strategic' determinants of its realization that lie beyond grand strategy and a common existential threat.

The actual political implementation and operational translation of multinational or 'common' transatlantic security beyond collective defense will depend in the first case, as it has become clear over the past few years, on national calculations - be they considerations of how to legitimate international military action in the face of their electorate, questions of the transfer of operational control to a multinational force commander or 'classical' attempts to maximize individual gains out of international cooperation at a minimized own contribution. This national dimension will now be analyzed in four examples, the United States, Great Britain, France and Germany.

2. United States: Multilateralism and National Prerogative

Like the aftermath of World War II, the end of the Cold War brought the U.S. into a paradoxical situation between the search for a peace dividend and the necessity to react to new, largely unforeseen challenges and threats.[2] Soon after 1945, they had realized that they were not to face a new world order but for the first time in their history a genuine world-political adversary, the Soviet Union with its Eurasic bloc, which had lead to a twofold political response. In terms of *moralpolitik*, the U.S. responded by propagating the idea of the 'free Western World' (as in the Truman doctrine of 1947), accompanied by a populist anti-Communism as it found its expression for example in the McCarthy era. In terms of *realpolitik*, the response was the set-up of a worldwide system of alliances or treaties and military bases to literally fence the

Eurasic Communist bloc (policy of containment), accompanied by a special not only militarily but also socio-economically defined umbrella for Western Europe (the latter formed by the OEEC, the later OECD).[3]

Now, after the end of the Cold War, hopes of a new world order have once again been disappointed and the vision shattered that the U.S. would now at last no longer have to resort to power politics but be able to replace the policy of containment by one of enlargement, spreading democratic values and practices.[4] But once again after the demise of the old, a new, if diffuse, opponent emerged. It forms around the risks of nuclear proliferation, drug dealing, ethno-national conflict constellations, militant so-called 'crazy states' and the hard to predict developments in the rim areas of the former Soviet bloc (for example South-Eastern Europe, Korea, China/Taiwan).

In terms of *realpolitik*, the response to these new security challenges could easily be derived from the logic of containment, transformed into a strategy of trying to fence a 'generalized' enemy and enhanced by the needs of international burden-sharing. In this regard, when discussing the strategic changes in U.S. security policy after the Cold War, its one actually outstanding epochal shift is away from unilateral self-commitment to European affairs and the strategic bondage to the 'old' continent after World War II, through the Atlantic Alliance. This trend however has not just begun with the final collapse and disappearance of the Soviet block but has been perceivable since the beginning of the Bush presidency. As RAND analyst Robert Levine observed, President Bush preferred rather taking "pragmatic centrists" like James Baker, Lawrence Eagleburger, Richard Cheney, Paul Wolfowitz and Brent Scowcroft into the foreign and security key positions of his administration than pronounced "Old Nationians" such as Alexander Haig, Caspar Weinberger or Fred Iklé, let alone "long-range NATO philosophers" like Henry Kissinger or Zbigniew Brzezinski.[5] However, at the same time, Levine argued that Europe and NATO would despite remain the chief reference points and spheres of interest for the U.S. for the years to come and went on concluding: "Washington's European orientation implies that the rest of the world, even Japan, and in the long run even the Middle East, will remain secondary in a security sense."[6]

Still, the slackening bipolar overlay over Europe lead to a paradoxical fundamental change in the U.S. approach to that region. According to its Wilsonian 'Make the world save for democracy' tradition, the United States early embarked on an enlargement strategy towards Eastern Europe. This was, at least in its beginning, not so much a strategy of 'tough' organizational expansion (such as NATO enlargement) but rather an approach based on Article 4 of the North Atlantic Treaty, calling for the spread of democratic values and procedures.[7] This more cooperative and less 'expansionist' approach was closely accompanied by a legitimatory enterprise, directed not only to one's own electorate but also to some Alliance member states that were seeking to slash their defense expenditures and to minimize substantial contribution to NATO budget and force requirements.

The clue to tie all together was found in creating the "security metaphor"[8] of 'new threats', mainly posed by the aforementioned 'generalized' enemy. That approach however increasingly equated 'democratic' value enlargement with geographical Alliance enlargement and thus in some minds activated the traditional U.S. military entanglement trauma. Namely,

> expansion would convert an alliance designed to achieve clear and limited security objectives in a relatively stable Cold War setting into a nebulous crisis-management organization in a highly unstable post-Cold War setting. NATO would change from a defensive alliance to protect the territory of member states from attack into an alliance to project force - a different mission with a vastly different set of risks and obligations. Even if the formal membership of the alliance were not increased, the de facto extension of NATO security jurisdiction eastward would be fraught with danger. NATO would become entangled in an assortment of disputes among the Central and East European states, many of which have the potential to explode into armed conflict at any time. Given the fragile nature of some of those nations, the alliance could even become mired in a number of internecine struggles.[9]

Given dire prospects of that kind, it was a logical consequence that once the Cold War era of immediate legitimate security interests in Europe was over, the U.S. changed to the mentioned approach of democratic value enlargement, by now having become synonymous with Alliance enlargement, at the same time seeking, to a certain degree, a strategic de-coupling from the European continent. The clearest sign of this latter trend is the CJTF concept officially approved at NATO's Ministerial Meeting in Berlin of June 1996 and the related decision to establish the core of European Defense and Security Identity within NATO structures yet, whenever desired, to be conductible under political leadership and responsibility not of the Alliance but the WEU.

Already the Clinton administration's definition of national security strategy makes it clear enough that in the post-strategic U.S. defense and security perimeters, Europe has become but one region among others, and possibly more important ones. The Clinton administration started off looking for a whole system of "integrated regional approaches" as the primary frame of reference for security policy, so that the U.S. as a "genuinely global power" would be able to realize its national interests within loose, multilateral forms of international cooperative action.[10] This however must not foreclose the option for unilateralism when circumstances require so. As the already mentioned Presidential Decision Directive (PDD) 25 of 4 May 1994, a kind of elementary doctrine for post-strategic security policy, states:

> When our interests dictate, the U.S. must be willing and able to fight and win wars, unilaterally whenever necessary. To do so, we must create the required capabilities and maintain them ready to use."[11] Even given those principles, the Clinton administration clarified that "circumstances will arise, however, when multilateral action best serves U.S. interests in preserving or restoring peace. ... Thus, establishment of a capability to conduct multilateral peace operations is part of our National Security Strategy and National Military Strategy.[12]

As for engagement in multilateral peace operations, this approach calls for a post-strategic security multilateralism in the sense of ad-hoc coalitions, utilizing common assets and operative frames, subject to ad-hoc activation according to the situation and one's own interests. The approach is thus exactly compatible with the CJTF concept. As for U.S. national strategy, "multilateral peace operations" are regarded as "an important component",[13] yet the President made it clear that "first, and foremost, our national interests will dictate the pace and extent of our engagement"[14]. Accordingly, deciding about the "When and How" of U.S. armed force deployments in multinational contexts will always remain a Presidential prerogative.[15]

Consequently, two principles emerge. Firstly, multilateral peace operations will only find U.S. support if they serve its immediate national interests and secondly, there will be no transfer of operational command over U.S. forces to a multinational force commander. Only necessary parts of operational control may be transferred:

> The President retains and will never relinquish command authority over U.S. forces. On a case by case basis, the President will consider placing appropriate U.S. forces under the operational control of a competent UN commander for specific UN operations authorized by the Security Council. The greater the U.S. military role, the less likely it will be that the U.S. will agree to have a UN commander exercise overall operational control over U.S. forces. Any large scale participation of U.S. forces in a major peace enforcement mission that is likely to involve combat should ordinarily be conducted under U.S. command and operational control or through competent regional organizations such as NATO or ad hoc coalitions.[16]

In the light of these principles, two scenarios for U.S.-supported multinational security engagement remain realistic: either a coalition of NATO countries authorized by a UN Security Council resolution, such as the UNITAF mission to Somalia, or the IFOR/SFOR model, as realized in Bosnia, with NATO and non-NATO countries conducting a joint operation, using common NATO assets and NATO command and control structures, with a U.S.-lead NATO Major Subordinate Command taking the strategic lead - as AFSOUTH in the case of IFOR.

U.S. peace and security engagement policy is determined to reassure that the peace operation in question will follow well-defined political and military aims, can be realized at a sensible cost/outcome-relation and, most importantly, that its success will be sustainable in a long-term view.[17] These regulations are clearly informed by the Vietnam syndrome. Accordingly, the U.S. Army Field Manual 100-23 - quite different from Great Britain and Germany for example - does not build upon the concept of wider or robust peacekeeping but on effective restoration of political order and stability in crisis regions, military enforcement of UN sanctions and setting up safe havens in cases of civil war-type crises.[18]

This realpolitik-laden cogent response to post-strategic security challenges aside, it becomes obvious that finding a related idealpolitik-guided response that also could bring specific content to the so stressed notion of the 'national interest' is of considerable difficulty. In the first place, this is due to the tradition of "moral pragmatism", a politico-philosophic conviction already harshly criticized by Hans J. Morgenthau.[19] It aims to overcome the tension between realpolitik and idealpolitik by seeking to unite the diverging traditional leading motives of U.S. foreign and security policy, which are "power, freedom and diplomacy"[20], within a broad overarching political disposition. Behind these three coin concepts stand the fear of becoming encircled by a Eurasic bloc, of an entanglement, namely an unwanted political and above all military fixation in regional constellations, and the resulting insight that for the sake of the United States' integrity and welfare it is sometimes necessary to intervene in conflicts and engage in a balance-of-power game even when, at first sight, no U.S. interests seem to be at stake.

Since 1990, various conceptions have tried to take all these aspects into a comprehensive account. Among them are the plead for an exclusive idealpolitik according to which not the balance of power but the "spread of freedom" should be the final aim;[21] the idea of a politics of "soft" or "co-optive power", basing on the power of ideas and the indirect, intentional realization of political interests, thus mainly aiming to reconcile real- and idealpolitik;[22] or - on the background of the experiences with Iraq, Somalia and former Yugoslavia - the concentration on regional "pivotal states" from which a kind of new domino effect may take its course, insofar regional balances shattered by them could also have a global destabilizing effect.[23] Now as before, a practicable post-strategic security doctrine, underpinned with concrete political content beyond shorthand abstraction from single-chase experience, is yet to be devised.[24]

3. Great Britain: From Defense to Security

British military doctrine shows distinct features of the Anglo-Saxon legal and also political culture with its emphasis on custom and precedence, that is, it typically arises not from conceptual planning but from agglomerated decisions and events.[25] Concerning multilateral peace operations, such principles basing on example cases are yet to form. Even until 1992, security policy found itself almost equated with wider national self-defense and defined in terms of four conventional aims: maintaining a nuclear deterrent capacity, defending Great Britain, contributing to West European defense and the defense of the East Atlantic and the Channel.[26]

Great Britain, like France, has only lately begun to undertake the step from defense to security, which also comprises an orientation away from unilateral and towards multilateral action in situations of crisis.[27] Quite different from Germany's position and comparable to that of the U.S., Britain thus articulates no self-reliant interest in securing international peace and stability. In contrast, it for a long time still emphasized the strictly national character of security interests and consequently derives three core functions of future British security policy: defending British territory, warding off threats to national and Alliance-wide security and contributing to wider national security interests in the sense of maintaining a benign international environment of peace and stability.[28]

Not until the Defense Estimates of 1995[29] can one witness a change in that policy, making it better corresponding to the changed global setting. Now the following security functions are considered: Maintaining an independent nuclear capacity,[30] adapting to NATO's new force structure[31] and taking part in humanitarian missions as well as the "Provision of a Military Contribution to Operations Under International Auspices"[32]. It looks as if this is a revival of the "dual stance" doctrine as it was developed after World War II and envisaged a double standing leg in defense and security affairs. The dual stance doctrine acknowledged Britain's demise as a world power at its strategic dependency on NATO, vice the U.S., but at the same time attempted to maintain a genuinely British standing leg in defense affairs and defined it - following the idea of global post-imperial British responsibility - in terms of the ability of unilateral military intervention virtually all around the world.[33] Reviving this tradition, already the 1994 Statement on the Defense Estimates had started with declaring that the United Kingdom disposes of one of the most splendid capacities of worldwide military force projection, only reached by the U.S., Russia and France.[34]

In contrast, because of Britain's undeniable strategic dependence on NATO assets and therefore on the U.S. (or, turned positive, because of the British-U.S. special relationship), the Atlantic Alliance has since its existence officially been regarded as an important framework for cooperative multinational action. Additionally, its importance is increased by the fact that the majority of the British security elite sees essential advantages in Britain exclusively engaging within the NATO framework as far as multilateral peace operations are concerned - and needless to say that Britain is to take over some of the decisive military command positions in these contexts.[35] British politicians well realize that they could not win only half as much political influence in the EU or WEU as they did in NATO. Through the transfer of the command over the ARRC for example, Britain gained the opportunity to have a part of its national command an control structure financed by NATO, with the opportunity left to use them, as well as the assigned British troops, for unilateral national operations almost as it pleases. That way, the revived dual-stance principle can not only be sustained in times of shrinking military budgets but also in the face of the necessity to lastingly take some army troops in the planning for domestic peace operations (for example Northern Ireland).[36]

Important to notice, therefore, British defense policy orientation toward NATO must not be confused with a mulitlateralization of national interests. Contributing to multilateral peace operations are, like a multilateralism in defense and security policy, far from representing genuine guiding lines or aims for British politics:

> The goal of our security policy is to maintain the freedom and territorial integrity of the United Kingdom and its Dependent Territories, and the ability to pursue our legitimate interests at home and abroad ... Security defined in this way ... encompasses sustaining the rule of law ... and creating and preserving the conditions of peace and stability in which we can pursue our national interests. ... British interests will best flourish, and our efforts produce the greatest returns, in a stable, humane an law-abiding world. ... In an interdependent world, many of our interests are shared with our partners and allies, in the United Nations, NATO, and the European Union. Indeed, many interests can sensibly only be pursued through multilateral institutions.[37]

Now as ever, Britain thus shows no interest in a sharing of sovereignty in the field of defense and security affairs. Recurrent British objections against the plan to make the WEU into an integral part of the envisaged ESDI therefore have come as no surprise. Comparable to the position of the U.S., Britain underscores the necessity to calculate in terms of the national interest. Consequently, military contributions to multinational peace operations will always be made on a selective base, which leaves no realistic alternatives to ad-hoc formed multi-state coalitions, typically within NATO.

In contrast to the U.S. however, Britain is not anxious to design international peace operations in a large-scale fashion that promises to secure its success in advance. Rather, it tends to prefer medium- and small scale operations because its colonial experience shows how difficult it can be to come to political terms with the long-term consequences of massive military engagement in crisis regions.[38] Accordingly, military planning for out-of-area operations concentrates on the tasks related to "wider peace-keeping" and contingency planning typically centers on measures of conflict prevention, demobilizing, military protection of civilians and humanitarian relief.[39]

There is however another, not officially mentioned reason for this orientation. Britain still maintains some overseas forces (in Cyprus, Central America and Gibraltar), but these are suited for little more than short-term and intensity operations.[40] Moreover, the Falkland War of 1982 underscored Britain's ability to unilaterally conduct out-of-area operations yet at the same time, and quite different from the above mentioned assertion, showed considerable problems with long-range force deployment and transportation, especially concerning air-lift.[41]

Finally, in the face of continued cuts in the defense budget and in the military forces volume, a broad operational engagement in a possible transatlantic security-multilateralism would, for the time being, not be a realistic political option anyway. Especially if Britain seeks to maintain its share in the defense planning for Europe, thus preserving the benefits stemming from its ARRC command, and at the same time remains resolved to continue its military presence in Northern Ireland, which requires a broad basis for personnel rotation, its out-of-area and short-of-war capabilities in general will be strongly limited over the next few years.[42]

4. France: New Interests in International Defense and Security Cooperation

France has been resistant to resigning of sovereign rights in the field of defense and security all along.[43] As it has not taken part in NATO's integrated military structure since 1966 and only recently started to consider a return, one should assume that, for the time being, the Atlantic Alliance is not a significant frame of reference whenever French military engagement short of war is at issue. Yet the opposite is true. Precisely because France seeks to avoid losses of national authority in defense and security affairs, it has tended since the beginning of the post-strategic security era to strongly relate to, and rely on, NATO (and not the UN, WEU or CSCE, respectively OSCE).

This is illustrated by the observation that while providing one of the largest personnel contingent for UN operations, France is always concerned to achieve the best possible congruence between the nations involved in conferring a UN mandate and those executing it. Ideally, this can be realized by the UN 'charging' NATO to implement a certain Security-Council sanction so that in consequence NATO states literally take themselves into duty,[44] as for example in the case of the IFOR and SFOR mission. Due to this interest in the Atlantic Alliance taking the lead of multinational peace operations, France had decided to take part again in Military Council sessions even before officially coming up with its consideration to return into NATO's military bodies in December 1995 - though only on an ad-hoc basis and as far as peace-keeping questions were concerned.[45]

The Atlantic Alliance is of prime importance to France for yet another reason. This is the *French security trilemma*. Three different security interests that are hardly consistent with one another form it. If they can be brought within some common context anyway, it is the one of NATO. To begin with, and as the first component of the dilemma, also the French political elite is convinced that only an enduring transatlantic Alliance makes European defense as well as short-of-war operations feasible. Related to this insight however is the apprehension that the U.S. may prefer a selective strategy as political approach to Europe to an integrative multilateralism. That would mean to look for different European cooperation partners, according to the situation, and that way not only undermine the emerging harbingers of a European Security and Defense Identity but also isolate France. The key event here was the Gulf War of 1991, during which French troops were placed under foreign (that is U.S.) command and control for the first time since 1966. France's role in the operation Desert Storm let the ambiguity of its traditional defense policy become obvious enough to trigger a national security debate.[46] National positioning in relation to NATO then definitively proved ambivalent, if not contradicting:[47]

Without a doubt, France is thrown dependent upon cooperation with, and assets of, the U.S. in the defense and security realm. The Franco-Atlantic bilateralism founded therein meets a broad national consensus. The Gulf War of 1991 however not only underscored Europe's, vice France's, strategic dependence on the U.S. but also conspicuously indicated that the U.S. were the only remaining genuine world power in terms of autonomy in defense affairs as well as material and general strategic capabilities. This, in the classical Waltzian sense, "shoved" France into a politics of counter-balancing that found its expression in the efforts to face the Euro-Atlantic security partnership once again with the conception of a relatively autonomous European pillar of NATO. The Copenhagen Ministerial Meeting of NATO in June 1991 provided an illustrative example. France forwarded a blueprint for a WEU-led rapid reaction force. Though it failed, an important transatlantic compromise was reached: In turn to the continued personal union between SACEUR (the Supreme Allied Commander in Europe) and CINCEUR (the Commander-in-Chief of the U.S. forces stationed in Europe), the U.S. agreed on the plan to elaborate the WEU into an integral part of a future European Defense and Security Identity. A plan however that after the Ministerial Meeting of Berlin in June 1996 and the final acceptance of the CJTF concept seems to have become somewhat obsolete and is now not only being objected by Britain but also by France itself.

The second component of the security trilemma arises from the two basic aims - Franco-American bilateralism and at the same time a European Security and Defense Identity or at least an autonomous European military pillar - being hard to combine and politically realize simultaneously, which however is decisive for abating the security trilemma. Both components cannot be reconciled but under the aegis of a continuous French rapprochement to the Atlantic Alliance. Therefore, France has a strong interest in establishing a form of European Security and Defense Identity which does not lead to a European uncoupling from the United States. France's, if so far unrealized, declaration of June 1996 not only to return into NATO's military committees but also to consider its full military reintegration was surely pushed forth by the North Atlantic Council's Berlin decision to explicitly task the WEU with setting up an own European defense capability on the basis of the CJTF concept. Accordingly, every decision about CJTF-based military engagement will be taken in the North Atlantic Council, which means unanimity and inclusion of the U.S., and as already mentioned, the (multinational) CJTF Headquarters will be available both to NATO and WEU, just as the assigned troops will be double-hatted, that is, answerable both to NATO and WEU.[48]

Additionally, as the trilemma's third component, French security policy seeks to obviate two threat scenarios at the same time, requiring different partners, respectively: Germany for guarding against a potential Eastern threat (of which, at least for some, Germany appears as a part) and Italy together with Spain and Portugal for handling the more manifest Southern threat as it results, among other things, from the legacies of colonialism. These twofold French post-strategic security interests become symbolically obvious the parallel interest in two different institutional forms: Eurocorps (with Germany as continental center power) and Eurofor/Euromar (with Italy, Spain and Portugal as Mediterranean countries vis-à-vis the North African crisis potential).

All these aspects, to sum up, resulted in a changed French policy towards NATO that combines elements of the transatlantic selectivity practiced sine 1966, when it had withdrawn from NATO's military integration, with elements of a new rapprochement.[49] First circumstantial evidence of these emerging trend could be observed since some time before the spectacular French decisions of December 1995 and June 1996. Taking part, for example, in the operation Deny Flight over Bosnia and the enforcement of the embargo against Serbia and Montenegro, French troops had indirectly returned into NATO's military integration months before.

This political change shows that by no means only Germany, as many have argued, sees itself faced with the necessity of redefining its role in common security policy. It applies as much to France and is also an interesting parallel to the British case that the end of bipolarity was synonymous with the end of traditional certainties in defense and security affairs. It is a suggestive example that France's political elite and opinion leaders have only since recently undertaken efforts to introduce the concept of 'international security (policy)' into common language. Only slowly growths the understanding of security politics being no national affair any more - and that it therefore cannot be practiced unilaterally by national defense politics but is becoming unimaginable without a sensible minimum of international integration. In this sense, already the Whitebook of 1994 carefully annotated it as "not unnormal" if French forces should assume a "more central" place in questions of (broadly defined) "collective security".[50]

5. Germany: The Dilemma of Double Normality

During the Cold War, a common coin-phrase said that the predominating national interest of the Federal Republic of Germany consisted in not having any, and there is still some truth in that. Common assessments of the current state of German foreign and defense policy along with corresponding recommendations draw it into the dilemma of *double normality*.[51] This dilemma arises from two commonly confounded but discrete and conflicting perspectives under which the united Germany may be examined and its international behavior judged. Viewed as a 'new' Germany, it is attributed increased political and military capabilities and obligations, whereas regarded as an enlarged 'old' Germany, it is expected to impose itself restraints and adhere to international expectations regardless of any own interests so to forestall any new raising fears of Germany[52].

In consequence, united Germany is sometimes seen as a "bigger and better" civilian power, abdicating any military engagement,[53] or in contrast as suffering from "Machtvergessenheit" (power oblivion) and falling prey to a universal multilateralism instead of following own national interests[54]. By some, moreover, it is viewed as a "great power with many options"[55], "ripening" geopolitically,[56] and being able, and capable, to chose autonomously the international way it desires. Others speak of a "new assertiveness"[57] and accuse Germany of desiring predominance in Europe, arguing in contrast to those seeing it as a "pressured power"[58] between a variety of incompatible international urges and expectations, between increased "opportunities" and "obligations",[59] leaving it no space to devise genuine national-interest and long-term conceptions.

Given these diverse assessments and predictions, the ending of Germany's constitutional special condition by the Federal Court's Bundeswehr sentence of July 1994 must not let forget that a genuine consensus about the envisaged multilateral action frames of German post-strategic security politics as well as about procedural questions (for example rules of engagement and questions of command and control transfer to a multinational force commander) is yet to emerge. According to the 1994 Whitebook, German vital national security interests consist, among others, in "a policy of networking and of fair balance in, for and with the community of nations."[60] In contrast to fairly common statements of that kind, also - or rather especially - after the Bundeswehr sentence a political guideline is indispensable that would contain general regulations for short-of-war military operations, transposable to the needs of actual missions in question. There is a whole spectrum of conceivable post-strategic peace operations. They may involve military action of different forms and grades and thus German decision-makers will have to decide which of those forms they favor so to sensibly derive the necessary and adequate financial, material and military contribution.

Quite different from these political shortcomings, the Federal Government and the Ministry of Defense early developed a political interest in participating, on an ad-hoc basis, in international peace operations. Accordingly, much effort was made to adapt national units to NATO's new force structure, with a special view to crisis reaction forces. Despite its world-community rhetoric and like the other countries examined here, Germany interestingly shows no decisive interest to actively contribute to UN peace operations on a large scale but concentrates on NATO-led operations.[61] An active contribution to NATO operations is seen to be an effective instrument to increase general German influence in the Alliance: "It is the aim to make an effective contribution to NATO's *crisis reaction forces* in particular, which is in keeping with Germany's role in the Alliance and establishes a qualified say".[62]

This nevertheless is not the effect of a sometimes maintained trend toward a creeping renationalization of German defense politics. Rather, it is the consequence of a specific cognitive scheme, or operational code of the German defense and security elite, largely informed by historical experience. It developed during the first years of West German rearmament (which started in 1955) on the grounds of the Federal Republic's nuclear dilemma. It consisted and still consists in the fact that Germany disposes of no nuclear weapons and thus has traditionally had difficulty in claiming a say in NATO strategy matters, sometimes even being about to lose step with the general strategic development of the Alliance.[63] Consequently, it has always been decisive to make an important non-nuclear contribution so to be indirectly able to claim a sensible say in pivotal strategic issues and moreover to try to anticipate the evolution of NATO's military strategy in order to adjust one's conventional contributions to it as well as possible. That is, in Wolfram Hanrieder's classical formulation, to strife for optimal international "compatibility".[64] Thus, "West German security policy became synonymous with Alliance policy. ... In international affairs, Germany assumed what might be called a 'instinctive multilateralism' ... Instead of pursuing specific national interests, West German security followed general aims."[65]

As a result, however, over the years the trauma emerged that almost ever when those compatibility decisions had just been taken with all the necessary domestic political debates and compromises and were about to be implemented, the international situation and NATO's strategic response would change, rendering Germany's adaptation efforts obsolete in large parts. Compare the following historical sketch:[66] After joining in 1955, every effort was made to set up a conventional defense capability that promised to make an adequate contribution to West European defense according to NATO's Lisbon Program of 1952. Yet shortly after beginning to levy the first Bundeswehr units, NATO's change from the conventionally based Lisbon strategy was beginning to be replaced by what in 1957 became NATO's new strategy of massive retaliation, widely known as MC 14/2. This caused Germany the need to make a hard turn in its just begun defense policy and force structure planning, and a flaming domestic debate about a nuclear arming of the Bundeswehr started. The plans for a nuclear armament of the Bundeswehr at first were well compatible with U.S. plans for a multilateral nuclear force (MLF). In 1964 however, the U.S. gave it up and Germany now saw itself compelled to join the now envisaged nuclear Nonproliferation Treaty (NPT). Into the bargain, NATO's Harmel Report of 1967 and the new strategy of flexible response, or MC 14/3, laid much emphasis again on conventional forces, the buildup of which Germany had postponed, expecting nuclear armament.

In the beginning post-strategic era, the complex of anticipated traumas caused new adaptation effects. This becomes widely obvious an a statement by General Naumann, then-Generalinspekteur of the Bundeswehr, who argued that "the Western Alliance not only offers security to our country but also creates ... far-reaching possibilities to influence the security policy of the partners. This is of vital interest for a non-nuclear nation like Germany".[67] Therefore, the reform of Bundeswehr structures, anyway necessary because of the integration of the former GDR's Nationale Volksarmee, was also used to adapt national force structures to NATO's new triad of basic organization, main defense forces and crisis reaction forces, as agreed in the Alliance's new Strategic Concept of Rome in November 1991. The result were German attempts often reprimanded as remilitarization to increase, or rather establish, basic national command and control capabilities for out-of-area and task force operations beyond individual and collective self-defense.[68] Nevertheless, this strategy did not show the desired positive effects.

One reason was that official German plans for an increased peace-keeping engagement obviously over-stretched the available resources and consequently risked, in the tradition of "Genscherism" (named after former Minister of Foreign Affairs Hans-Dietrich Genscher), to get stuck in the rhetorics of

"Verantwortungspolitik" (politics of responsibility) and a moral overcommitment.[69] Consequently, as Timothy Ash pointed out, "with increased demands on limited resources, the danger is that by trying to do everything Germany will end up achieving nothing."[70] Additionally, repetitive spontaneous cuts in the Bundeswehr's military strength and curbs in the defense budget, for several years accompanied by confusing domestic debates about the future scope, extent and mode of German 'peace politics' have partly led to the international perception that Germany after all is not really interested in broadening its role in the Atlantic Alliance and actually resuming more responsibility.[71] In fact, for the time being, Germany remains unable to command any peace support operations exceeding 20.000 troops.[72]

Despite its politico-historical peculiarities, Germany shares with the U.S., Britain and France three important principles for contributing to multilateral peace operations. First, decisions whether to take part or not will always be made on an ad-hoc basis and nationally.[73] Second, the deployed forces will remain under national command and control. Only operational control may be transferred to a multinational force commander or to a commander nominated by an international organization, for example the UN.[74] Third, planning is based on individual and collective self-defense as basic reference points.[75] Multilateral peace operations are seen as a broadening of this primary defense mission in the light of the changed world-political situation but not as a qualitatively independent dimension of security policy.

6. Consequences for the Policies of NATO Engagement and Enlargement

The ascertained predominance of national interest-calculations in post-Cold War Alliance politics and security engagement as it shines through the aforesaid three principles which *all* the countries examined here have in common is at first sight another instance of the continued appropriateness of (neo)realist reasoning. But at the same time, it shows that neorealism should open itself to insights provided by the less structuralist and more historico-political or textual approach as promoted by social theory and critical security studies. Well exemplifying the importance of the institutionalist principle of path-dependency, the tendency of renationalization in post-strategic security sometimes shining through can well be accounted for on the ground of what could be termed the *identity hypothesis*. This hypothesis suggests that the loss of a common existential threat has posed all high-stake players of the Cold War period into the predicament of redefining their roles and interests in the face of no common, 'objective' reference points. Consequently, by far not only Germany, but also the U.S. and others are compelled to find an appropriate way of self-positioning in the new security setting, which allows for much less structural, balance-of-power type, strategic and military capability-guided reasoning.[76]

Even if this should not lead one to subscribing to the over-sketched axiom of a totally de-objectivated "no-essentialist character" of security and security politics,[77] it a least underlines the fact that no nation can continue to define its security and security strategy on the grounds of a mere program of delimitation against well-defined, objective 'threats' and 'adversaries'. At the latest by now, it is up to (and incumbent on) each country of the Euro-Atlantic to "write" its security policy and security condition itself.[78] Post-strategic security politics then become, in some important aspects, interpretatory politics of identity.

Yet apart from those theoretical considerations, the relevance of the national dimension of Alliance politics has an important practical consequence concerning the question of adequate policy guidelines for the future role of an enlarging NATO. The suggestion is that NATO, in continuing its process of institutional adaptation and enlargement, should refrain from adopting too diffuse *political* responsibilities and claiming a too broad *functional* spectrum in post-strategic security politics. Both, in its fuzziness, could grow at odds with national peace-operation doctrines and cause some member states balancing behavior against each other, naturally at the expense of the Alliance's political as well as military integration and operativeness.

Such tendencies have already become obvious in the French case. The more France was stepping forth in its 'rapprochement' to the NATO's military integration, the more it became resolved not to politically tie itself too much to the Alliance. Hence it has been seeking to counterbalance perceptions of NATO's functional widening and 'politicization' by reinforcing its demands and attempts to build up some important pieces of the envisaged genuinely European Security and Defense Identity not within but parallel to the Alliance. This trend had become visible already before France announced its decision to consider a full return into NATO's military bodies. For example in the WEU's Petersberg Declaration of June 1992. This declaration, at least on paper, opened the door to autonomous West European military actions, reaching from blue-helmet peace-keeping to collective defense - beyond the Atlantic Alliance. Needless to say that such institutional duplications not only have negative effects upon common security policy within the Alliance but also upon multilateral peace operations. On the one hand, being outgrowths of national balancing behavior, they forestall any sustainable comprehensive solutions, whereas on the other, they may lead to uncoordinated political as well as military activities, consuming energy, straining common assets and conjuring up intra-Alliance conflict.

Moreover, as neorealist alliance theory could argue, NATO should in any case restrict itself to military tasks and common military politics in a comparatively narrow sense, so not to risk its *positive functional specificity* to wither away. Finally, it is exactly this functional specificity that has kept NATO attractive to its members, and arguably made it so attractive to its prospective members. As Henry Kissinger cautioned,

> The task before us is nothing less than to distill a sense of direction from a world in which almost all key elements are changing simultaneously. Stability in Europe requires reaffirming the centrality of NATO rather than diluting it in an abstract multilateralism.[79]

Any strategy seeking to assign NATO a prominent functional role in *any* question of post-strategic European security - from humanitarian concerns to collective defense and the vision of an all-regional system of collective security - has to be regarded with sincere reservations. The Alliance would risk drifting into a *mere* expression of common value orientations, de facto hovering in "desuetude".[80] That way, it may risk to become just another security-codex formulation agency with little effective value when it comes to a clash between the values proclaimed and the national interest:

> Consider the Budapest Document adopted at the December 1994 CSCE Summit. Its 'Code of Conduct on Politico-Military Aspects of Security' requires that when armed forces are used for internal security purposes that force be commensurate to the needs for enforcement and that due care be taken to avoid injury to civilians or their property. Only a few days after this CSCE Document was agreed, however, Russian forces began their alarming campaign in Chechnya, resulting in heavy civilian losses and hundreds of thousands of internally displaced persons.[81]

Hence, appreciating the principles put forward in the Study on NATO Enlargement[82], a firm caveat is in order, for the political strategy finally recommended therein to bring NATO on the course of enlargement indeed involves much of functional diffusion. Although the Study on NATO Enlargement was anxious to point out strategies (such as intensified military and peace-keeping cooperation and joint operations with the new members) to ensure that enlargement will strengthen the Alliance, it still in large parts seemed to conceive of NATO enlargement as a general political evolutionary process almost parallel to enlarging the European Union, with a common all-European zone of political and economic stability as the leading motive. Alliance enlargement, according to the study, shall lead to a new role of NATO as a complementary part of an "inclusive European security architecture" together with the OSCE.

These rhetorics aside, one must not forget that, as neorealist alliance theory suggests, the classical security dilemma can still today become interest- and policy-determining, though in the changed form of a not international-political but alliance-internal dilemma (being insecure about the allies' politics and how sustainable for example issue-specific cooperation with them will be).[83] If this is true, it is one more strong argument for NATO sticking to functional specificity. This necessity is underscored by some tendencies of a free fall in national defense readiness and overall NATO military capability already alluded to: "The NATO infrastructure budget has shrunk by 60 per cent in four years, and the NATO Defense Ministers warned on 15 December 1995 of 'shortfalls ... especially related to support for reaction forces, ground-based air defense and strategic mobility'."[84]

In the light of those arguments, David Carment's recommendation that "NATO's best strategy for legitimacy and effectiveness is to embrace the future as a leader in ethnic conflict prevention"[85] seems somewhat misguided. His envisaged "three-step process" would not only let NATO's functional specificity wither away but also deprive the Alliance of any specific meaning, vigor and assets that could keep it attractive to its members. Carment's recommendations include suggesting NATO to become active in various diffuse areas of conflict prevention: "assistance in guaranteeing the independence of each state; then eventually their integration into the West; and finally, embedding each state's institutions in broader pan-European institutions."[86]

Yet, much as the value of such a strategy is debatable, Carment clearly grasps the requirement for improved intra-Alliance political coordination as well as the national-interest dependency of overall Alliance effectiveness:

> NATO effectiveness will be only as good as its member states want it to be. Conflict prevention is an aspect of, not a replacement for foreign policy. Assigning of tasks to an international regime, even if that involves seemingly routinized activities, will be accomplished and sustained only if individual states believe that their interests are served best through that commitment.[87]

Together with predominating national-interest calculations and domestic constraints in the practice of short-of-war military operations, the absence of a common existential threat as well as the calls for a Re-Europeanization of European security (sounding from both sides of the Atlantic - in the U.S. case as an outgrowth of the calls for post-Cold War military disengagement, especially in possibly entangling conflicts, and in some European countries, especially France, in consequence of the objective to realize a genuine European security and defense identity) have brought about some tendencies of Euro-Atlantic alienation. "NATO's Bosnia Divide"[88] is the clearest example:

> The catalyst for the transatlantic dispute was the decision by the Clinton administration, in compliance with a legally binding decision by Congress, to withdraw militarily from enforcing the arms embargo against Bosnia. While the practical consequences of the U.S. decision to end enforcement of the international arms embargo against Bosnia were negligible, the unilateral move gave a new sharpness to the debate about the future of transatlantic cooperation in foreign affairs and defense. The order from President Clinton meant that

U.S. ships under NATO command in Operation Sharp Guard unilaterally disobeyed part of an agreed policy of the Alliance. Moreover, with the disengagement from the embargo U.S. forces ceased to pass intelligence concerning shipments in the Adriatic to the other allies. Finally, the decision undercut a NATO engagement to carry out a mandatory resolution of the U.N. Security Council to which the United States had given its approval.[89]

Domestic constraints of such kind are not only typical of the U.S., yet here they combine with a strong preference for an "à la carte approach"[90] to multilateral peace operations. This à la carte approach conceives of the Alliance's future role and of its enlargement in terms of enhancing an all-European cooperative spirit - which will rather exacerbate than alleviate the tendency from transatlantic burden sharing to "burden shedding"[91].

To steer against those drifts, *NATO should rather do a step back from than a step toward the vision of a general European security evolutionism* and concentrate on the dimension of conflict management *within* the Alliance itself, which will be of even increased importance after admitting new members. It is worth remembering what the Copenhagen Ministerial Meeting of 1991 concluded in this respect under the headline "The Nature of the Alliance":

> 2. NATO embodies the transatlantic link by which the security of North America is permanently tied to the security of Europe. It is the practical expression of effective collective effort among its members in support of their common interests.
>
> 3. The fundamental operating principle of the Alliance is that of common commitment and mutual cooperation among sovereign states in support of the indivisibility of security for all of its members. Solidarity within the Alliance, given substance and effect by NATO's daily work in both the political and military spheres, ensures that no single Ally is forced to rely upon its own national efforts alone in dealing with basic security challenges. Without depriving member states of their right and duty to assume their sovereign responsibilities in the field of defence, the Alliance enables them through collective effort to enhance their ability to realise their essential national security objectives.
>
> 4. The resulting sense of equal security amongst the members of the Alliance, regardless of differences in their circumstances or in their national military capabilities relative to each other, contributes to overall stability within Europe and thus to the creation of conditions conducive to increased cooperation both among Alliance members and with others. It is on this basis that members of the Alliance, together with other nations, are able to pursue the development of cooperative structures of security for a Europe whole and free.[92]

Adhering to functional specificity does not stipulate that the Alliance devote itself to seeking to redefine post-strategic defense and security politics into all-out war military strategy. In post-strategic security, military aspects of security in a broader sense by far not only refer to classical war scenarios or military intervention but also play an important role in peaceful management of internal conflict and democratic consolidation. Functional specificity in the area of the military dimensions of security thus

> includes the facilitation of transparency in national defence planning and the enduring democratic control of the armed forces. The expression 'democratic control of the military' is generally understood as the subordination of the armed forces to democratically elected political authorities; it means that all decisions concerning the defence of the country must be taken by those elected to take charge of the country's affairs. However, while there is general understanding of what the expression means, there is less agreement on how it should be achieved; what structures and procedures are necessary and, what role should be played by parliaments.
>
> There are a variety of reasons why it is important to professionalize the armies of Eastern and Central Europe. In conditions of internal instability, domestic strife or civil turmoil, the military can represent a relatively stable element and source of order. History is replete with examples where the military have assumed power or positions of dominance or have threatened to act in defiance of the government of the day. In these circumstances, the loyalty of the armed forces is a critical element. The fundamental assumption is that the armed forces are loyal to the democratically elected government of the day. However, constitutional arrangements sometimes leave a dangerous degree of ambiguity. Democratic political control is assured through a combination of process, structure and attitude. While there is no single model, there are several fundamental characteristics: a clear legal and constitutional framework; the hierarchical responsibility of the military to the government of the day through a civilian Minister of Defence; qualified civilians to work with the military in the elaboration of defence requirements and the agreement of defence policy and budget; the clear division of professional responsibility between civilian and military; and the effective oversight and scrutiny of parliament.[93]

Of course, this broader perspective on military functions in conflict management poses several questions and dilemmas as far as concrete forms of NATO peace operations are concerned. One is the much-discussed issue of *mission-creep*, a slow change in the character of a mission in progress so that it is growing at odds with its initial conditions and rules of engagement. This problem comes to the boil when the mission in question is a *NATO-plus mission*, that is, it includes non-members. In those cases, the initial common objectives and command and control arrangements will be the results of difficult international bargaining and, once agreed upon, a rather fixed matter precluding continual adaptation as the progress of the mission may require.

The best example here is the IFOR experience. IFOR as well as SFOR, its follow-up mission, not only was occupied with implementing the Dayton peace provisions but also creepingly developed into a general support agency for reconstruction activities in Bosnia that did not fall into its initial scope, such as repatriation, economic reconstruction or election monitoring.[94] In such cases, it will be difficult to unite historically shaped, divergent national interests in when, how and to what purpose participating in multilateral peace operations, as outlined above. As for IFOR, and SFOR, the two operations were only made possible by traditional NATO bodies as well as new institutional ramifications (NACC and PfP), although they were anything but designed for solving the various tasks that such a multilateral security engagement poses.

Divergent national interests in the face of concrete post-strategic security tasks again underscore the need for a continued focus on NATO military cohesion, operativeness and capability of short-term contingency planning and implementation. Consequently and somewhat against the thread of the present study, especially in the face of the coming enlargement process and its *political* implications, one should at least equally heed the *military* dimension and six principles which the Military Committee agreed upon in March 1994:

(1) Preserve the integrated military structure;
(2) Assure separable but not separate forces in support of the European Pillar;
(3) Maintain a single command structure for both Article 5 and non-Article 5 missions;
(4) Retain the role of the Military Committee in transmitting strategic guidance from the NAC [North Atlantic Council] to NATO military authorities;
(5) Avoid ad hoc participation in NATO bodies; and
(6) Preserve the capability of the Major NATO Commanders to undertake timely contingency planning.[95]

As mentioned above, after a time of functional diffusion and catch-all security rhetorics, NATO's Berlin Ministerial Meeting of 1996 marked a clear reorientation to functional specificity and thus was an important step to realizing those six principles. The related section in the Final Communiqué reads:

> In our adaptation efforts to improve the Alliance's capability to fulfil its roles and missions, with the participation of all Allies, we will be guided by three fundamental objectives.
>
> The first objective is to ensure the Alliance's military effectiveness so that it is able, in the changing security environment facing Europe, to perform its traditional mission of collective defence and through flexible and agreed procedures to undertake new roles in changing circumstances ...
>
> The second objective is to preserve the transatlantic link ...
>
> The third objective is the development of the European Security and Defence Identity within the Alliance. Taking full advantage of the approved CJTF concept, this identity will be grounded on sound military principles and supported by appropriate military planning and permit the creation of militarily coherent and effective forces capable of operating under the political control and strategic direction of the WEU.[96]

Chapter Six
Alliance Engagement under the Post-strategic Condition

1. Euro-Atlantic Security Multilateralism: Path-Dependency vs. Mastery

Now the praxeological question remains which form of international cooperation in post-strategic security politics appears realistic in the light of the findings presented here. And in addition: What will be the most feasible and likely institutional form of future Euro-Atlantic security relations? Also here, a genuinely institutionalist perspective may help, as the one provided by the newly developed approach of "multilateralism"[1]. When seeking to forestall the appearing trend of à-la-carte post-strategic security, basing upon ad-hoc decisions in the wake of national self-interests, a multilateral-institutional approach offers itself as a suitable mid-term conception.

In contrast to pure national self-interest directed ad-hoc cooperation on the one side or fully 'communalized' security politics on the other, *security multilateralism* appears as a realistic and stable meso-integrative political form and operational framework. It bears respect of important national reservations and prerogatives, at the same time overcoming the narrow limits of mere case-dependent cooperation in security affairs. Thus, it could make a valuable contribution to crafting the Atlantic Alliance for its political and operational future in the era of post-strategic security. Within such a multilateral security community, some important common procedures and shared interests would emerge, and there would also be well-attuned national and multinational decision-making procedures in concrete questions of prospective military operations, as well as clear rules of engagement.

Yet at first it is necessary to recall that international security in general and European security in particular can no longer be conceived of in solely *structural* terms, as some prominent theoretical approaches continue to do. It cannot sensibly be seen as a well-defined problem of the international distribution of state capabilities (as according to structural realism), as an iterated, continuous game of sensitizing adaptation and enlightenment of short-term national interests to some common political goals, thus establishing some more lasting structures of inter-state cooperation on the grounds of crescent reciprocity in state action (as according to neoliberalism), or as a pure coordination problem in the wake of commonly perceived global threats and emerging world interests, rendering national interests and state strategies more and more irrelevant (as according to normative theory).

Looking at the new European security puzzle, to reiterate what has been suggested above, security has become a fuzzy multi-level and multi-context problem, being on its best way to involve real security *politics* and not merely questions of military strategy and strategic bargaining. *Selective multi-state cooperation in changing coalitions* will become both typical of and crucial for NATO's continuing relevance and effectiveness. This requires on the side of the member states the willingness and ability to (re)define their relations to NATO and with one another from issue to issue. A security multilateralism will entail *different coalitions within the Alliance*, as the case may be, for example for the provision of common defense, for conflict-intervention in implementation of UN resolutions or for humanitarian assistance.

All the benefits of such an approach notwithstanding, it will be difficult to define clear common assets and strategies for the Atlantic Alliance as such. Consequently, any successful common management of post-strategic security challenges will be likely *to require a certain level of intentional renationalization* in Western defense politics. Paradoxical as this may seem, only then, for instance, can the approach of 'broad security' and 'coalitions of the willing' within the CJTF-framework be implemented. NATO's members (and cooperation partners) need to define military assets available for multilateral action, especially provisions for the transfer of operational control to a multinational force commander and a special focus on military, and 'political' interoperability. Otherwise, NATO's comprehensive approach to security in the new Europe will suffer from a growing gap between idea and implementation.

Methodically speaking, also in the question of a feasible post-strategic European and transatlantic security multilateralism, heeding the principles of historical path-dependency, conceptual as well as political discontinuity and multiple causation opens important insights. Foremost, such a perspective reminds us to bear two characteristics of post-strategic security in action. *First, the organization and structure of peace operations to a large part have a contingent character.* They developed on occasion of and evolved along case by case contingencies, their special nature, the related international interests in their settlement and the organizational context available shorthand.

Peace-keeping is the best example. Originally a realistic de facto amendment to the UN Charter so to reflect the condition of bipolarity which made the realization the collective security system as envisaged in Chapter VII of the UN Charter unlikely, it has become one of the outstanding forms of conflict management, also in the post-Cold War era. That is, it has become institutionalized and thus comparatively insensitive to the change in its initial conditions of existence. And, in consequence, it has conquered the minds of many statesmen and international organization officials so that it would not be easy to discard as inappropriate to the typically protracted conflicts in the post-bipolar world, as opposed to the more contingency-type conflicts during the Cold War. Peace-keeping still is a prevailing political idea, even given the UNPROFOR debacle ending the UN peace-keeping mission in ex-Yugoslavia and calling upon the Atlantic Alliance to provide relief to the attacked blue-helmets and subsequently to implement the Dayton peace accord.

Second however, in the post-Cold War era, institutional structures of international cooperation also in the security realm are, if with variations, remarkably stable and will provide some effective leading norms and legitimizing potential for post-strategic security engagement. The other side of this is that, in contrast to the post-World War II situation, the post-Cold War setting does not allow for a new beginning in terms of institutional foundation from scratch. Quite different from postmodernist critical theory's recommendation, overcome historico-political textures thus cannot simply be abolished, but we have to try to adapt them as well as possible to the changed conditions in which they now are to operate and hopefully function. There is no option of setting up a new global system of security, a kind of world polity, as idealistically advocated by the internationalists of the normative theory school.

A report from the Stockholm Peace Research Institute (SIPRI) elaborated, albeit the through-shining disappointment about the loss of a master-plan vision, some of the remarkable positive aspects of the post-Cold War European security condition:

> Fundamental to the new security environment is the fact that, by the end of 1995, 30 states parties to the Treaty on Conventional Armed Forces in Europe (CFE Treaty) had reduced their heavy weapons by more than 50 000 items in the Atlantic-to-the-Urals area. Along with the Russian troop withdrawals from Central Europe and the Baltic states which were completed in 1994, this created an unprecedented core of military stability and predictability in Europe. The OSCE Forum for Security Cooperation and the 1994 Code of Conduct on Politico-Military Aspects of Security promoted a new type of relationship among European states based on cooperative approaches to security. The record of implementation of the Vienna Document on Confidence- and Security-Building Measures is improving, with more states providing more complete information on different types of military activity; efforts to address regional, subregional and sub-state confidence- and security-building are gaining momentum. In addition, preventive measures, crisis management and other forms of peace mission are supplementing traditional arms control approaches in shaping the new cooperative regime.
>
> These developments have been accompanied by the spread of a system of common values across Europe. The post-communist states are increasingly adhering to the principles of democracy and political pluralism, market economics and the rule of law. Their commitment to respect international standards in the field of human rights and fundamental freedoms has paved the way for the admission of most of these states to the Council of Europe. Many of them also aspire to membership of both NATO and the European Union (EU).
>
> Furthermore, they have made considerable strides towards settling problems in their mutual relations in the form of international treaties. A significant step in

> this process was the March 1995 signing in Paris of the Pact on Stability in Europe, which was then transmitted by the EU to the OSCE for follow-up and implementation in close cooperation with the Council of Europe.
>
> Clearly, the post-cold war security system is emerging as the result of a host of ad hoc and sometimes contradictory practical steps. While this system could simply be allowed to develop haphazardly, our view is that it is desirable to attempt to shape its framework and to determine its direction. However, it will not evolve according to a single 'master design'; it will emerge gradually through a process of trial and error rather than through the implementation of model-based approaches. Ultimately, the fundamental task is to effectively manage the risks and meet the challenges of the new security environment in Europe.[2]

Whereas the SIPRI report felicitously grasped the path-dependent and often piecemeal development of the hazy foundations of a future European security order, which definitely foreclose grand institutional design-type solutions, it seemed a bit too gloomy about the chances to intentionally influence at least some dimensions of the related institutional and political developments.

From the institutionalist perspective advocated here, a more adequate outlook on the development of Euro-Atlantic security and security cooperation seems to be the one of an "institutional evolutionism", which in a medium-term perspective does not assume any security organization to take the political or military-operative lead but rather a steady interplay at a medium level of international security integration and political coordination.[3] *Security community then will more be provided for by shared norms, rules and interests than by a specific organizational framework.*

The formation of a common European and transatlantic post-strategic security community will thus neither follow a "master plan" nor a mere "trial and error"-principle[4] but developmental paths shaped by national interests and prerogatives *as well as* institutionally solidified fundaments (for example the Atlantic Alliance as an organized institutional form, the Euro-Atlantic Partnership Council and CJTF as institutional amendments and common historico-political experiences within IFOR or SFOR in Bosnia). In the end, it will always be crucial how the qualities and capabilities of cooperation and integration reached up to a certain point of time proof effective (or not) in the light of *concrete* security challenges. This kind of *single-case* utility principle of *general* cooperation and integration has already manifested itself especially in the development of the CJTF-concept with its emphasis on multinational headquarters cells and multinational-multifunctional forces. This concept unexpectedly and unpredictably well fitted the requirements posed by the decision to set up the multinational IFOR and SFOR troops with their strong so-called *NATO-plus* requirements, namely coordinating a combined operation of

NATO and non-NATO countries and establishing the necessary command and control structures.

One can hence expect a kind of *dual system of European and transatlantic security* to emerge within NATO. The first of the two interdependent components forming it would be a sufficient defense capability for the case of classical geostrategic threats, reflected in suitable forms of high-level military co-operation and integration - keeping in mind that the related command and control structures at the same time also represent the preconditions of conducting effective multinational operations precisely beyond collective defense and short of war. The second component would consist in sufficiently institutionalized forms of selective and graded reaction to sub-strategic security challenges or support tasks for UN operations.[5]

This also seems the only viable solution to the problem of *mission creep*, that is a stepwise, hard to notice and therefore 'creeping' change in the initial situation or tasks of a military peace operation or conflict intervention so that they consequently either come into obvious contradiction to the original political and operational rules and goals of the mission or at least hamper its progress and effectiveness. Ad-hoc arrangements cannot reach the capacity for steady adaptation required here, just because the political preconditions, complementary initial interests and compromises that actually made the operation possible must not steadily be questioned and redefined. General, evolved and adaptive but nevertheless institutionalized rules of engagement forming a kind of *NATO doctrine for post-strategic NATO operations* - be they conducted in implementation of UN resolutions, by NATO as such or by state coalitions using some NATO assets - could help defuse this problem.[6] The CJTF-conception could again serve as a good organizational background.

The decisive national prerequisite for a security multilateralism to emerge and also for a successful implementation of the CJTF conception will be, in addition to a sustainable internal-political compromise about national decision-making procedures and political objectives, creating suitable military capabilities, especially concerning secured international interoperability in the sense of "complementary militaries"[7]. Moreover, these need to be employable not only multi*laterally* but also multi*functionally* - from peace-keeping to genuine military operations. Defense and force planning then would have to change from the still ascertainable conceptual primacy of individual and collective self-defense toward the whole spectrum of possible military operations in the service of post-strategic security, that is, it should center on multilateral responses to cases of "'complex emergency'".[8]

2. A Final Word: What NATO Should Not Do

Practically, post-strategic security engagement in complex emergencies will often be synonymous with conflict management in a broader sense. *This, however, is not to say that NATO Alliance politics need to become politics of conflict management so to preserve the North Atlantic Alliance's relevancy and appropriateness. The opposite may be true.* So far as the role of NATO in post-strategic, complex emergencies is concerned, several caveats are in order here, grounded mainly in the specific structure of those conflicts. To begin with, their causes will be largely of inner-societal nature, as it has already become evident over the past few years in the case of ethno-national conflicts.[9] As it has also become clear, there is a historically remarkable international consensus among virtually all actors about the general imperative of international conflict management. This general consensus is contrasted by the lack of a modal and instrumental consensus. That is to say, the different opinions about how those interventions should be designed and which instruments should come to use are hardly congruent. Moreover, communicative processes in a broader sense are likely to play a dominant part in the violent escalation of conflict as well as in the international concern with the conflict (that is, how it is depicted in the mass media) and subsequent de-escalating attempts. That makes geostrategically based solutions for protracted conflicts, especially ethnic ones, hard to implement and sustain. This entails an important consequence for future NATO peace operations in a broader sense.

Judging from the IFOR and SFOR experience, NATO has been growing somewhat into the role of what may be called a robust interposition force and peace-keeping agency, also considerably contributing to coordinating and supporting the work of an almost inestimable lot of civil aid and reconstruction organizations and activities. So it could be tempting, also with a view to the Alliances political outreach to Central and Eastern Europe and the coming enlargement process, to see its most important role to come and strongest potential for continued legitimacy in the public in exerting such coordinative functions as a lead-organization. *Such an approach, however, is already dubious in that it is likely to regularly involve difficulty that is beyond the scope and control of the Alliance but for which it finally may be held responsible despite.*

However, a more sincere reservation concerns the territorial approach of political geometry as a strategy for conflict management. The example of former Yugoslavia shows that such formal strategies are not quite promising in coping with escalated ethno-national conflict. It is a fact that ideologies and propaganda cannot be done away with just by means of a kind of *ethnogeometry*. This term refers to the attempt to resolve protracted ethnic conflicts (which have their roots not in superficial and short-term discrepancies of interests but in whole incompatible images of the world, commitments to values etc.) by means of the geographical separation of the conflicting parties. The lines of this separation however will always tend to be arbitrarily defined, as will be the newly constructed areas of ethnical homogeneity. What makes ethno-geometry a flaw right from its start is its overlooking that deeply rooted ethnic conflicts will always grow exuberantly across territorial lines of demarcation, safe havens, or areas of settlement - and be it just as an effect of telecommunicative dispersion. This problem comes to the boil when, after the fading of Communism as their main source of power and legitimization, local elites resort to ethno-national agitation as a strategy for their political survival. However, already territorial separation as such may lead to exacerbation. In a long term perspective, it typically will turn out as dysfunctional because it forecloses almost any kind of communication-related conflict resolution, thus helping to open the door for reciprocal misperceptions and the development of chronified negative stereotypes.[10]

Generally, though complex conflict management being likely to become one of NATO's primary operational occupations in the years to come, less likely to involve traditional military than increasingly 'political' decisions and functions (for example acting as a lead-organization, as just noted), one should not argue for a full 'politicization' of the Alliance. Such a politicization would be rendering the Alliance's operational stance increasingly ineffective and also increasingly invisible - thus undermining the benefits of post-strategic deterrence, nor for an operational 'hyper-flexibility'. In the final analysis, both will dissipate the Alliance's image and strength as a widely visible integrated security organization. It is precisely that operational hard core and institutional visibility beyond strategic myths or mere "representational politics"[11] of imagined-identity construction that NATO has so much invested in over the decades and that has, in retrospective, always turned out to be the driving force not only for its own continued integration and general relevance but also for the future course of transatlantic and European security, with important effects on the European political condition as a whole.

Chapter Seven
Conclusion and Outlook

NATO's specific *long-standing functions* enshrined in the Articles 2, 4 and 5 of the North Atlantic Treaty, such as providing for broadly-defined regional security, forming a reliable international milieu for projecting political and economic stability or serving as a framework for developing sustainable peaceful and stable relations between its member states, have remained remarkably unquestioned and even been reaffirmed by the system-change in Europe 1989-91 and its aftermath. Article 2 is of special importance here. It reads:

> The Parties will contribute toward the further development of peaceful and friendly international relations by strengthening their free institutions, by bringing about a better understanding of the principles upon which these institutions are founded, and by promoting conditions of stability and well-being. They will seek to eliminate conflict in their international economic policies and will encourage economic collaboration between any or all of them.

However, much of NATO's procedures and politics seeking to fulfill these functions and realize these aims now as before are to be redefined and where necessary redesigned due to the changed political setting and scope in and under which the Alliance is operating now. The clearest signs for this need are the various meetings held by the North Atlantic Council, which were to a lower degree concerned with questions of goal-setting than they were with the problem of how to adapt the Alliance's political and military organization so to keep the goal-attainment processes effective. *Primarily, NATO had, and still has, not to redefine its functional role but its operational prerequisites to comply with it.*

There are, of course, also several relevant questions relating to *goal setting*. In the first place, whereas during bipolarity the pivotal issue was how to maintain Alliance relevancy and effectiveness through *unity and integration*, now it is how to maintain Alliance relevancy and effectiveness through *multiplicity and differentiation*. That not only reflects the new political shape of Europe and corresponding new national interests of NATO's member states but also the specific character of the post-strategic security challenges the Alliance is and will be facing. The step is in the latter respect one from common to graduated reaction according to the functional needs posed by each single case in question, involving more and more *political*, as opposed to military-operational functions. The challenge is not to plunge into an à-la-carte ad-hocery here.

Looking at the *national dimension* of NATO's adaptation and prospects revealed especially interesting insights, both for theory and practice. All four countries examined (United States, Britain, France and Germany) agree in that they subject their support of all multilateral peace operations likely to involve military action to three main criteria, which center on the primacy of national interests and not of enlightened, internationalist kind - as for example the global governance school, normative theory and some branches of the neoliberal paradigm suggest. Firstly, the decision whether to take part or not will always be taken from one case in point to the next. Secondly, no national command and control authority will be transferred, except for limited operational control arrangements (which is a clear rejection of any supranational form of security community). Thirdly, main reference point for military planning remains national security and national or collective self-defense. International peace operations are not regarded as an end in itself or as a distinctive political obligation.

The findings further suggest that after the dissolution of the bipolar overlay, national security policy is more conditioned by *historical* than *systemic* pressure. Thus, research should concentrate on the "culture of national security"[1]. Here are some important findings in this respect:

The position of the U.S. towards international peace operations is characterized by the principles of multilateralism and Presidential prerogative. The envisaged platforms for action are regionally disposed, multilateral frameworks which can be activated according to the situation and operational needs. NATO is but one option among others. Given its traditional fear of entanglement, the U.S., after the vanish of a common existential threat, hold strong reservations against any option-restricting, lasting one-side commitments and rigorously maintain that any use of their military forces always has to promote their immediate national interests. If conducted, multinational military operations should be of a scale that offers a realistic chance of fast and sustainable success - a distinct reflection of the Vietnam syndrome.

Great Britain has only recently taken the conceptual step from defense to security policy. The Defense Estimates of 1992 for example still followed this tendency only hesitatingly and - like the U.S. - subordinated any political decision to support multilateral peace operations with British troops strictly to calculations of national interest. On the other hand, Britain has clearly recognized the payoffs of international cooperation in security affairs and of Alliance integration. And also in contrast to the U.S., Britain favors not so much massive military actions as a wider peace-keeping, involving moderate use of military force and being foremost political in nature.

France now as before regards an elaborated multilateralism of international peace and security engagement and the related possible losses of national decision-autonomy with skepticism - even given its rapprochement to NATO's military structures. However, like in Britain, the prevailing notion of national and Alliance defense has since recently been on its way to become enlarged towards security policy in a general sense. NATO has become an important reference point in this respect, at least in consequence of realizing one's own continued strategic dependence on Alliance (vice U.S.) assets as well as following the reform of the Alliance's military structure, which well enough corresponds to French interests (for example the CJTF concept).

Germany still has not taken up a clear position in the field of post-strategic security. Now as before, diffuse set phrases predominate, centering on "increased international responsibility", "politics of responsibility" or the now realized "capability to act in foreign and security" on a sound constitutional basis. Unlike the impressions left by the quick and uncontroversial decision to take part in IFOR and SFOR, the underlying procedures for taking and justifying before the electorate those kinds of Bundeswehr deployment decisions still seem fragile. Furthermore, despite a national force structure and equipment planning intent to make a valuable contribution to NATO's new category of crisis reaction forces, Germany still lacks a policy-conception that would define specific interests, objectives and the envisaged military 'intensity' of an engagement in different conceivable forms of multilateral peace operations.

Especially, recent developments in German security policy and its self-envisioned role in NATO cannot be explained just by resorting to common (neo)realist, neoliberal or intergovernmentalist axioms such as (respectively) securing its relative position in the international system, devising enlightened, internationalized interests or playing two-level games between domestic and international win sets. Rather, analysis should try to grasp the typical *problématique* of its subject. As the question of the factors forging the ambiguous appearance of German security policy in the 1990s makes clear, historico-cultural, political-psychological and perceptional co-determinants have to be taken into account (such as the tradition of West-German security thought on the background of the nuclear dilemma and the problem of Germany suddenly being expected to define for itself a military role, whereas having been restricted and internationally encouraged to a multilateralized international status of low profile, at least in military terms, ever since it joined the Alliance).

France also provides an interesting example in terms of theory. France's rapprochement to NATO commenced right *after the vanish* of the old and void of a new obvious threat. Even if it so far has not led to a full reintegration into the Alliance's military structures, it more than questions the gloomy Mearsheimerian vision of a Balkanized Europe with NATO fading away and an upcoming 19th century-like concert of renationalized foreign and security politics.

Another point is that with the multifunctional and multilateral CJTF approach (consciously envisioning alliances within the Alliance precisely for the sake of NATO's cohesion in the face of post-strategic security challenges), postmodern-critical theorists no longer can see NATO's future depending on the question if it (or rather the U.S.) will succeed in committing the allies to a new grand collective approach of transatlanticism so to downplay any national differences.

The findings altogether constitute an important argument against the theoretical schools of global governance and neoliberalism. The predominant norms governments adhere to when undertaking international action, at least in the realm of security and conflict management, typically are not international democratic norms or political principles set out in the charters of international organization and enforced by an attentive world-public. In contrast, they typically stem from national calculations, mainly in terms of historical experience, that is, historically instructed operational codes.

This makes a strong case for *foreign policy analysis*, even in an era of increasingly multilateralized foreign and security politics and is thus a strong argument for the continued adequacy of (neo)realist thought. However, so far as neorealism still adheres to Waltz-type structural realist reasoning, it should acknowledge an important insight from the preceding analysis: *Not international-political pressure ('shoving' a unit to striving for maintaining its current 'position' in the international system and seeking to aggrandize its 'security') but historical pressure based on interpreting one's own history seems to trigger all of the examined national security policies determining the scope of feasible Alliance engagement in the post-strategic setting.* That amounts to suggesting a combination of structuralist and constructivist reasoning.

Further on, *units do not - as structural realism still maintains - react uniformously to international-political change.* To reiterate, especially as concerns conflict management, peace-keeping and peace-enforcement, the different units' responses are mainly conditioned, again, by the historical dimension, making them path-dependent in the institutionalist sense. This becomes nicely obvious in the case of current national peace-keeping and peace-enforcement doctrines, be they implicit or explicit, which are clearly informed by remembrances of colonial interventions back in the respective nations' history as well as more recent all-out-war engagement (Vietnam in the U.S. case or the Gulf War of 1991 in the French) and conclusions drawn from related operational difficulty and final successes and failures. The 'cultural' dimension in a broader sense apparently not only plays a prominent role in devising the security interests of a civilian power and Mittelmacht such as Germany but also in the case of traditional major (military) powers.

The examples adduced here also stand both for the necessity of an integrated institutional perspective on European security (with path-dependency, discontinuity and multiple causation as methodical pillars) and the missing of a serious institutional approach or a common institutional theory of international politics. That considerable deficit provides the chance of overcoming the currently dominating, however fashionable stylization of theoretical differences and uniting especially neorealist and neoliberal thought within a common overarching, multi-method frame of reference.

The current *neorealist-neoliberal debate* about international institutions, in contrast, neither contributes to refining institutional analysis nor will it lead to, but at best hamper the development of a serious institutionalism in International Relations. From an institutionalist vantage point as put forward at the outset of this study, *the question often enough is not one of neorealism vs. neoliberalism, neither one of traditionalism vs. critical social theory, but one of adequately bringing them all in with their respective strengths according to the problem in question.* Whereas neither neorealism nor neoliberalism alone have proven to be capable of an adequate institutional analysis, some important neorealist and neoliberal concepts, placed into an overarching framework, turned out to be useful and promising analytical tools for conceptualizing institutional change.

Notably, by far not only *neoliberal* assumptions (such as saving on transaction costs or rectifying sub-optimal outcomes of cooperation) can explain why states may seek continued cooperation, for example in alliance contexts, under conditions of missing international-political structural pressure in the sense of Waltz[2]. *Neorealist* alliance theory for instance assumes that precisely the loss of the common enemy or threat perception can trigger convergence in the members' national security politics. This is an effect of the intra-alliance security dilemma, which becomes virulent whenever security "collaboration" in the face of a common existential threat becomes, as a consequence of the virtual disappearance of that threat, security "coordination"[3]. On the one hand, alliance cohesion decreases, whereas on the other, the regulation of genuinely *political* questions increasingly defines the cooperation agenda. In such a situation of course, the allies' behavior becomes far less predictable and calculable than it used to be during the times of a structural overlay posed by a common military threat. Neorealist alliance theory assumes that to mitigate this so to speak 'political' security dilemma, member states will change to a strategy of intra-alliance balancing and counter-balancing so that the different national security policies will be approaching one another over time - and finally come considerably closer than in the wake of a common external threat. Like this, particularly the French *rapprochement* to NATO's military integration can be explained more cogently than by neoliberal assumptions.

Suggesting a general proposition, *alliances surviving the collapse of their - explicit or implicit - adversary tend to gain the character and typical problems of a security community* along with sharply defined military threat vanishing. Then the question of internal political mechanisms gains decisive significance, leading up to the just mentioned intra-alliance security dilemma, which seems to become dominant whenever alliances cease to be counterbalancing instruments and develop into security alignments in a broader, institutional sense. What appears decisive for the future of NATO then is to a lesser extent its organized *structure* (for example strategic assets) than its historically developed *character* (or quality) as a Euro-Atlantic security *institution* with sets of informal rules, expectations, common interests, routinized procedures, and a so to say world-public image - enhanced by the outreach to the former Warsaw-Pact countries and the coming enlargement.

An overarching institutional perspective could also unite the neorealist and neoliberal approach to post-strategic international cooperation. Within such a broader framework, *neoliberalism*, according to the findings presented here, could especially contribute to understanding and explaining the (continued) need for cooperative structures. Thereto it appertains to sharpen the analytical and political sight for the literal polymorphy of international cooperative structures, which large parts of neorealism still will obstruct, for they continue to conceive of alliances, and thus also of NATO, as mere defense pacts. However, NATO in particular distinguishes itself by a multiple institutional sub- and outbuilding. It is formed, for instance, by integrated headquarters, amending cooperative agreements and consultative bodies (such as PfP, the former NACC or the newly founded EAPC) as well as an own institutional representative, the Secretary General. This institutional structure however, and here *neorealism's* strength comes in, offers the member states various opportunities to articulate and pursue national interests. In this context, neorealist approaches could make an important contribution to explaining and predicting the concrete shape and contents of institutionalized cooperative forms in their specific functionality.

Institutionalist methodology as advocated here offers important tools for checking the process of NATO's institutional adaptation for its underlying causes, comparatively checking related theoretical assumptions and finally devising a forecast and recommendation for the future shape and organization of post-strategic security in Europe. Yet one important caveat is in order: Institutionalist methodology, by its very name, must not disguise that *many of the problems encountered in setting up a European security architecture and placing NATO in that structure are not problems of institutions and their relationships but problems of the nations belonging (or, as in the case of the Russian factor, even not belonging) to those institutions.*

As regards *policy guidelines for the future of NATO*, as underscored in the preceding chapter, *one should neither argue for a full politicization of the Alliance nor for an operational hyper-flexibility*. Over-politicization may result in rendering the Alliance's military component not only progressively ineffective but also increasingly invisible - thus undermining both the benefits of post-strategic deterrence and many members' interest in continued integration. Hyper-flexibility, for example in the wage of the CJTF-concept, surely would contribute to short reaction times and increased defense capabilities to meet uncertain and locally dispersed risks but also dissipate the Alliance's image and strength as a widely visible integrated security organization. However, it is precisely that *operational hard core and institutional visibility beyond strategic myths or mere representational politics of identity construction* that NATO has so much invested in over the decades and that has, in retrospective, always turned out to be the driving force not only for its own continued integration and general relevance but also for the future course of transatlantic and European security. And this all the more as it caused debates and strains both within the Alliance and the broader pan-European context - just to mention the NATO crisis of 1966-7 and the adoption of the strategy of flexible response or, needless to say, the 1979 crisis, that is the double-track decision and subsequent debates about its consequences and implementation.

The troublesome shaping process of a post-strategic European and transatlantic security structure is an outstanding example of the path-dependency of political institution-building and adaptation. What especially marks the post-strategic security realm as distinct is the foreclosed option of a clear institutional 'new' beginning, for almost all of the institutional forms of the Cold War era survived the vanishing of its founding conditions and were quick to adopt, or at least declare the adoption of, new responsibilities and functions. *This makes it unrealistic, as it will still be undertaken sometimes, to seek to construct and realize an all-comprising European security structure based on clear-cut functional differentiation and alleged 'synergy' between the existing institutions.*

It seems as that we will have to live with a *new security paradox*: The 'new' internationally relevant conflicts seem to denounce the state-centric model insofar as they are precisely of sub- or transnational origin. Security politics apparently cannot any longer be equated with strategy, geopolitics or a world of nation-states. In fact, as international politics in general, it has ceased to be a "tournament of distinctive knights"[4]. Yet at the same time, as experience from Somalia to former Yugoslavia suggests, the typical contemporary contingencies only can be effectively countered with recourse to capabilities and strategies particular to the nation-state system. This leaves security studies and politics alike in a predicament.

Finally, the once criterion of NATO's success, that is not to make operational use of its assets, now seemingly muted into a danger for its continued relevance. Moreover, whereas some forty years of joint NATO planning for military contingencies mainly considered all-out war scenarios and the ability to collective crisis-response, in the coming era of post-strategic security the

Alliance will see itself faced with a continued situation of smaller contingencies. During the first forty years of its existence, the main rationale for revising its strategic concept and military structure was to build upon deterrence and, thus, decreasing the likelihood of the necessity of crisis-response and use of its integrated military structure. After the vanish of a common existential military threat however, NATO can only retain its rationale and "alliance relevancy"[5] by restructuring with a view to operatively use its assets and military force - a case which only a decennium ago would have hinted upon its ultimate failure as a deterrent.

So NATO's role in post-Cold War Europe is, and will remain, in part paradoxical from a historical perspective - which is a necessary consequence of its political and military successes and institutional adaptability. The problématique of the system-change in Europe and the emerging post-strategic condition, in its theoretical and practical consequences for the future role of the Atlantic Alliance, is fuzzy and multi-layered and does not allow for final solutions, political or theoretical. For almost half a century, NATO and its members have successfully lived and acted under various world-political and Euro-regional conditions, and the Alliance has made indispensable contributions to regional and transatlantic, as well as arguably global, cooperation and stability, by far not only defined in military but also in general political terms. This it owed in the first place to the prudent politics of its member states' governments and finally prevailing willingness and ability to make constructive compromises.

To maintain this ability and preparedness well beyond the threshold of the next century together with the related reciprocally attuned values, interests and modes of behavior, sustainably embedding the new members into them, will be the greatest challenge and chief test for the Alliance's stance in the new Europe.

Endnotes

Chapter One: L'OTAN est morte, vive l'OTAN! - Fictions, Facts and Challenges

1. Harry Summers, "What is War," *Harpers* 268 (1984), No. 1608, pp. 75-8 (p. 75).
2. Madrid Declaration on Euro-Atlantic Security and Cooperation. Issued by the Heads of State and Government participating in the meeting of the North Atlantic Council in Madrid on 8th July 1997 (NATO Press Communiqué M-1[97]81, 8 July 1997), para. 6.
3. Ibid., para. 8.
4. See Michael O'Hanlon, "Transforming NATO: The Role of European Forces," *Survival* 39 (1997), No. 3, pp. 5-15.
5. See Escott Reid, *Time of Fear and Hope. The Making of the North Atlantic Treaty 1947-1949* (Toronto: McClelland and Stewart, 1977), pp. 18-9 and 99-112.
6. See Francis H. Heller and John R. Gillingham, eds., *NATO: The Founding of the Atlantic Alliance and the Integration of Europe* (New York: St. Martin's Press, 1992).
7. Cf. Charles L. Glaser, "Why NATO is Still Best. Future Security Arrangements for Europe," *International Security* 18 (1993), No. 1, pp. 5-50.
8. Cf. Bradley S. Klein, "How the West was One: Representational Politics of NATO," *International Studies Quarterly* 34 (1990), pp. 311-25.
9. See John F. Duffield, "NATO's functions after the Cold War," *Political Science Quarterly* 109 (1994/95), pp. 763-87.
10. In May 1997, the countries of the North Atlantic Cooperation Council and participating countries of the Partnership for Peace agreed to establish the Euro-Atlantic Partnership Council (EAPC), replacing NACC and broadening its scope. The EAPC, among other things, serves as an overarching framework for consultations and activities within PfP. See Basic Document on the Euro-Atlantic Partnership Council (NATO Press Release M-NACC-EAPC-1[97]66, 30 May 1997).
11. See Peter Schmidt, *Germany, France and NATO* (Carlisle, PA: U.S. Army War College, Strategic Studies Institute, 1994), pp. 12-3.
12. As intermediate accounts for the continued role, changing shape and new roles of NATO after the Cold War, see Ted G. Carpenter, ed., *The Future of NATO* (London: Cass, 1995); Walter Goldstein, ed., *Security in Europe: The Role of NATO After the Cold War* (London: Brassey's, 1994); Philip H. Gordon, ed., *NATO's Transformation. The Changing Shape of the Atlantic Alliance* (Oxford: Rowman and Littlefield, 1997); Robert A. Levine, ed., *Transition and Turmoil in the Atlantic Alliance* (New York: Crane Russak, 1992); S. Victor Papacosma and Mary Ann Heiss, eds., *NATO in the Post-Cold War Era: Does it Have a Future?* (New York: St. Martin's Press, 1995).
13. See Robert P. Grant, "France's new relationship with NATO," *Survival* 38 (1996), No. 1, pp. 58-80; Anand Menon, "From independence to cooperation: France, NATO and European security," *International Affairs* (London) 71 (1995), pp. 19-34.
14. See Paul A. Chilton, *Security Metaphors. Cold War Discourse from Containment to Common House* (New York: Peter Lang, 1996), pp. 357-402.
15. Ibid., pp. 357-402.
16. See Philip Zelikow, "Foreign Policy Engineering: From Theory to Practice and Back Again," *International Security* 18 (1994), No. 4, pp. 143-71.

17. Gianni Bonvicini et. al., eds., *A Renewed Partnership for Europe* (Baden-Baden: Nomos, 1995/96).
18. Robert A. Levine, *NATO, the Subjective Alliance: The Debate Over the Future* (Santa Monica, CA: RAND, 1988).

Chapter Two: Theoretical Accounts for NATO's Adaptation and Prospects

1. As examples, see the following comprehensive volumes: Mike Bowker and Richard Brown, eds., *From War to Collapse: Theory and World Politics in the 1980s* (Cambridge: Cambridge University Press, 1993); Ernst-Otto Czempiel and James N. Rosenau, eds., *Global Changes and Theoretical Challenges. Approaches to World Politics for the 1990s* (Lexington, MA: Lexington Books, 1989); Yosef Lapid and Friedrich Kratochwil, eds., *The Return of Culture and Identity in IR Theory* (Boulder, CO: Rienner, 1996); Richard Ned Lebow and Thomas Risse-Kappen, eds., *International Relations Theory and the End of the Cold War* (New York: Columbia University Press, 1995); Geir Lundestad and Arne Westad, eds., *Beyond the Cold War: New Dimensions in International Relations* (Oslo: Scandinavian University Press, 1993).
2. See Helga Haftendorn, "The Security Puzzle: Theory-Building and Discipline-Building in International Security," *International Studies Quarterly* 35 (1991), pp. 3-17 (p. 3).
3. Ibid., p.3. See also the reflections presented in Ronnie D. Lipschutz, ed., *On Security* (New York: Columbia University Press, 1995).
4. See Alexander L. George, *Bridging the Gap. Theory and Practice in Foreign Policy* (Washington, D.C.: U.S. Institute of Peace, 1993).
5. Fred Halliday, *Rethinking International Relations* (Houndmills: Macmillan, 1994), p. 6.
6. James Lee Ray and Bruce Russett, "The Future as Arbiter of Theoretical Controversies: Predictions, Explanations and the End of the Cold War," *British Journal of Political Science* 26 (1996), pp. 441-70 (p. 446).
7. See already Ken Booth and Nicholas Wheeler, "Contending philosophies about security in Europe," in Colin McInnes, ed., *Security and Strategy in the New Europe* (London: Routledge, 1992), pp. 3-36.
8. For the latest readers, see David A. Baldwin, ed., *Neorealism and Neoliberalism. The Contemporary Debate* (New York: Columbia University Press, 1993) and Charles W. Kegley, ed., *Controversies in International Relations Theory. Realism and the Neoliberal Challenge* (New York: St. Martin's Press, 1995). For thoughtful critics of that debate and its intellectual limitations, see Richard W. Mansbach, "Neo-This and Neo-That: Or, 'Play It Sam' (Again and Again)," *Mershon International Studies Review* 40 (1996), pp. 90-5; Robert Powell, "Anarchy in international relations theory: the neorealist-neoliberal debate," *International Organization* 48 (1994), pp. 313-44.
9. For a comparison of the according neorealist and neoliberal propositions, see Joseph M. Grieco, "Anarchy and the limits of cooperation: a realist critique of the newest liberal institutionalism," in Baldwin, ed., *Neorealism and Neoliberalism*, pp. 116-40 (pp. 133-4).
10. In their efforts, Hellmann and Wolf overlooked the fact that both schools of thought have less to say something about the future of the Atlantic Alliance *itself* (or its further organizational and functional development) than about the future behavior of its member states and the likely future of intra-Alliance cooperation. Cf. Gunther Hellmann and Rein-

hard Wolf, "Neorealism, Neoliberal Institutionalism, and the Future of NATO," *Security Studies* 3 (1993), pp. 3-43. These restrictions also apply to the newer theoretical account for NATO's recent development provided by Robert McCalla, "NATO's persistence after the cold war," *International Organization* 50 (1996), pp. 445-75.

11. Sometimes it seems as if it still has neither filtered through that not only Waltz-inspired neorealism makes up the contemporary neorealist paradigm nor that it is far from being typical of the neorealist paradigm's response to the international-political change after the Cold War. For other important neorealist trends and branches, see for instance Barry Buzan, Charles Jones and Richard Little, *The Logic of Anarchy. Neorealism to Structural Realism* (New York: Columbia University Press, 1993) and Benjamin Frankel, ed., *Realism. Restatement and Renewal* (London: Cass, 1996). These however are beyond the progressively myopic scope of the neorealist-neoliberal debate.

12. See Kenneth N. Waltz, *Theory of International Politics* (New York: McGraw-Hill, 1979), pp. 118-22 and 126. For a recent reformulation of this axiom see for example John J. Mearsheimer, "The False Promise of International Institutions," *International Security* 19 (1994/95), No. 3, pp. 5-49 (pp. 9-14).

13. See Waltz, *Theory of International Politics*, pp. 91-2.

14. See Mearsheimer, "The False Promise," p. 13.

15. See Grieco, "Anarchy and the limits of cooperation," p. 335.

16. See Glenn H. Snyder, "The Security Dilemma in Alliance Politics," *World Politics* 36 (1984), pp. 461-95; Glenn H. Snyder, "Alliance Theory: A Neorealist First Cut," *Journal of International Affairs* 44 (1990), pp. 103-23.

17. Founding works are Robert O. Keohane, *After Hegemony. Cooperation and Discord in the World Political Economy* (Princeton, NJ: Princeton University Press, 1984) and Robert O. Keohane, *International Institutions and State Power. Essays in International Relations Theory* (Boulder, CO: Westview, 1989).

18. Keohane, *International Institutions*, pp. 1-2.

19. Keohane, *After Hegemony*, p. 85.

20. See ibid., pp. 85 and 88-106.

21. Keohane, *International Institutions*, p. 8.

22. Thus the sum-up of what neoliberal institutionalism has revealed so far (that is, in some ten years) sounds somewhat poor: "Institutions sometimes matter for state policy, but we do not adequately understand in what domains they matter most, under what conditions, and how their effects are exerted. More research on this subject, by students of world politics critical of institutionalist theory as well as by those working from it, is essential and will be most welcome." See Robert O. Keohane and Lisa L. Martin, "The Promise of Institutionalist Theory," *International Security* 20 (1995), No. 1, pp. 39-51 (p. 50).

23. Cf. Keohane, *International Institutions*, p. 2.

24. Cf. Robert O. Keohane, "The Analysis of International Regimes. Toward a European-American Research Programme," in Volker Rittberger, ed., *Regime Theory and International Relations* (Oxford: Clarendon, 1993), pp. 23-45.

25. Cf. Keohane, *International Institutions*, p. 15.

26. Cf. Robert O. Keohane, "Institutional Theory and the Realist Challenge after the Cold War," in Baldwin, ed., *Neorealism and Neoliberalism*, pp. 269-300 (pp. 273-4).

27. For an exception, see Ingo Peters, ed., *New Security Challenges: The Adaptation of International Institutions. Reforming the UN, NATO, EU and CSCE Since 1989* (New York: St. Martin's Press, 1996).

28. See the critics by William Wallace, "European-Atlantic Security Institutions: Current State and Future Prospects," *International Spectator* 29 (1994), No. 3, pp. 37-51 (p. 45).

29. See Keohane, "Institutional Theory," p. 295 (emphasis added).

30. See ibid., p. 271.

31. Mearsheimer, "The False Promise," p. 18.

32. See Rey Koslowski and Friedrich V. Kratochwil, "Understanding change in international politics: the Soviet empire's demise and the international system," *International Organization* 48 (1994), pp. 215-47 (p. 227).

33. See Peter B. Evans, Harold K. Jacobson and Robert D. Putnam, eds., *Double-Edged Diplomacy. International Bargaining and Domestic Politics* (Berkeley, CA.: University of California Press, 1993) as well as the results presented in Thomas Risse-Kappen, ed., *Bringing Transnational Relations Back In. Non-State Actors, Domestic Structures and International Institutions* (New York: Columbia University Press, 1995).

34. See James B. Steinberg, *Overlapping Institutions, Underinsured Security: The Evolution of the Post-Cold War Security Order* (Santa Monica, CA: RAND, 1993).

35. Major works include Barry Buzan et. al., *The European Security Order Recast. Scenarios for the Post-Cold War Era* (London: Pinter, 1990); Barry Buzan et. al., *Identity, Migration and the New Security Agenda in Europe* (New York: St. Martin's Press, 1993); Ole Wæver, Pierre Lemaitre and Elzbieta Tromer, eds., *European Polyphony: Perspectives Beyond East-West Confrontation* (New York: St. Martin's Press, 1989). For a review, see Bill McSweeny, "Identity and Security: Buzan and the Copenhagen School," *Review of International Studies* 22 (1996), pp. 81-93.

36. These are Buzan, Jones and Little, *Logic of Anarchy*.

37. See Buzan et. al., *Identity*, p. 189; Ole Wæver, "Securitization and Desecuritization," in Lipschutz, ed., *On Security*, pp. 46-86 (pp. 57-75).

38. Hellmann and Wolf, "Future of NATO," p. 4.

39. The founding work is often regarded to be Nicholas G. Onuf, *The World of Our Making. Rules and Rule in Social Theory* (Columbia, SC: University of South Carolina Press, 1989). Important contributions include Hayward Alker, *Rediscoveries and Reformulations. Humanistic Methodologies for International Studies* (Cambridge: Cambridge University Press, 1996); Mark Hoffman, "Critical Theory and the Inter-paradigm Debate," in Hugh C. Dyer and Leon Mangasarian, eds., *The Study of International Relations. The State of the Art* (New York: St. Martin's Press, 1989), pp. 60-86; Koslowski and Kratochwil, "Understanding change"; Richard Ned Lebow, "The long peace, the end of the cold war, and the failure of realism," *International Organization* 48 (1994), pp. 249-77; Justin Rosenberg, *The Empire of Civil Society. A Critique of the Realist Theory of International Relations* (London: Verso, 1994); Jan Aart Scholte, *International Relations of Social Change* (Buckingham, PA: Open University Press, 1993); Alexander Wendt, "Constructing International Politics," *International Security* 20 (1995), No. 1, pp. 71-81; Alexander Wendt and Raymond Duvall, "Institutions and International Order," in Czempiel and Rosenau, eds., *Global Changes*, pp. 51-73.

40. Typical Works include Roger Carey and Trevor C. Salmon, eds., *International Security in the Modern World* (New York: St. Martin's Press, 1992); Neta C. Crawford, "Once and Future Security Studies," *Security Studies* 1 (1991), pp. 283-316; Michael T. Klare and Daniel C. Thomas, eds., *World Security. Challenges for a New Century* (2. Ed., New York: St. Martin's Press, 1994); Bradley S. Klein, "After Strategy: The Search for a Post-Modern Politics of Peace," *Alternatives* 13 (1988), pp. 293-318; Bradley S. Klein, *Strategic Studies*

and World Order (Cambridge: Cambridge University Press, 1994). See also the overview by Keith Krause and Michael C. Williams, "Broadening the agenda of security studies: Politics and methods," *Mershon International Studies Review* 40 (1996), pp. 229-54.

41. Cf. for example Wendt, "Constructing International Politics"; Wendt and Duvall, "Institutions and International Order".

42. Cf. the contributions in Lapid and Kratochwil, eds., *Return of Culture*.

43. Cf. McCalla, "NATO's persistence," pp. 456-61.

44. Inis L. Claude, jr., *Swords Into Plowshares. Problems and Progress of International Organization* (4. Ed., New York: McGraw-Hill, 1984), p. 267.

45. Contributions include James G. March and Johan P. Olsen, *Rediscovering Institutions. The Organizational Basis of Politics* (New York: The Free Press, 1989); James G. March and Johan P. Olsen, *Institutional Perspectives on Political Institutions* (Oslo: The Research Council of Norway, 1994); Walter W. Powell and Paul J. DiMaggio, eds., *The New Institutionalism in Organizational Analysis* (Chicago, IL: University of Chicago Press, 1991) as well as Gunnar Grendstad and Per Selle, "Cultural theory and the new institutionalism," *Journal of Theoretical Politics* 7 (1995), pp. 5-27; John Ikenberry, "Conclusion: an institutional approach to American foreign economic policy," *International Organization* 42 (1988), pp. 219-43; Thomas A. Koelble, "The new institutionalism in political science and sociology," *Comparative Politics* 27 (1995), pp. 231-43. Especially for international relations, see James A. Caporaso, "International relations theory and multilateralism: the search for foundations," *International Organization* 46 (1992), pp. 599-632; John G. Ruggie, ed., *Multilateralism Matters. The Theory and Praxis of an Institutional Form* (New York: Columbia University Press, 1993).

46. In the sense of Richard Little, "International Relations and the Methodological Turn," *Political Studies* 39 (1991), pp. 463-78.

47. On this multiple and variable context-dependency, see Koelble, "The new institutionalism," pp. 234-5; March and Olsen, *Institutional Perspectives*, p. 16.

48. See also Caporaso, "International relations theory and multilateralism," p. 620-30; Ikenberry, "Conclusion," pp. 223-6.

49. See Caporaso, "International relations theory and multilateralism," pp. 627-8.

50. See Wendt, "Constructing international politics"; Koslowski and Kratochwil, "Understanding change," p. 247.

51. Koelble, "The new institutionalism," p. 235.

52. March and Olsen, *Institutional Perspectives*, p. 14.

53. Waltz, *Theory of International Politics*, p. 108.

54. For a different argument against the grand-design approach, see Paul Cornish, "European security: the end of architecture and the new NATO," *International Affairs* (London) 72 (1996), pp. 751-69.

55. March and Olsen, *Institutional Perspectives*, pp. 16-7.

Chapter Three: The Global Dimension of NATO's Relevance, Role and Future

1. The following section draws from Helga Haftendorn, "The Security Puzzle: Theory-Building and Discipline-Building in International Security," *International Studies Quarterly* 35 (1991), pp. 3-17, Volker Rittberger and Michael Zürn, "Transformation der Konflikte in den Ost-West-Beziehungen. Versuch einer institutionalistischen Bestandsaufnah-

me," *Politische Vierteljahresschrift* 32 (1991), pp. 399-424 and my *Neorealismus, Neoliberalismus und postinternationale Politik* (Opladen: Westdeutscher Verlag, 1997), pp. 217-23.

2. Where (classical) realism and its multi-faceted descendant, neorealism, make comparable statements, which are thus typical of general realist thought in international relations, this study will employ the label *(neo)realist* to cover both.

3. For a general, introductory account of those and other theoretical schools mentioned here and henceforth, see Scott Burchill and Andrew Linklater, *Theories of International Relations* (Houndmills: Macmillan, 1996).

4. Almost a classic here is of course Kenneth N. Waltz, *Theory of International Politics* (New York: McGraw-Hill, 1979). See also, as one example of many newer treatments of relevance for the following, the discussion in Charles W. Kegley and Gregory A. Raymond, *A Multipolar Peace? Great-Power Politics in the Twenty-first Century* (New York: St. Martin's Press, 1994), pp. 18 and 46-50.

5. See Barry R. Posen, "Security Dilemma and Ethnic Conflict," in Michael E. Brown, ed., *Ethnic Conflict and International Security* (Princeton, NJ: Princeton University Press, 1993), pp. 103-124.

6. The concept of "overlay" is introduced in Barry Buzan et. al., *The European Security Order Recast. Scenarios for the Post-Cold War Era* (London: Pinter, 1990).

7. As discussed above, see ch. 2.1.

8. Examplary texts are compiled in James N. Rosenau and Ernst-Otto Czempiel, eds., *Governance Without Government: Order and Change in World Politics* (Cambridge: Cambrige University Press, 1992).

9. See Bruce Russett, *Grasping the Democratic Peace. Principles for a Post-Cold War World* (Princeton, NJ: Princeton University Press, 1993), p. 11.

10. Mayor works include Richard A. Falk, Robert C. Johansen and Samuel S. Kim, eds., *The Constitutional Foundations of World Peace* (Albany, NJ: State University of New York Press, 1993); Kjell Goldmann, *The Logic of Internationalism. Coercion and Accommodation* (London: Routledge, 1994); Lynn H. Miller, *Global Order. Values and Power in International Politics* (3. Ed., Boulder, CO: Westview, 1994).

11. See Robert C. Johansen, "Toward a New Code of International Conduct: War, Peacekeeping, and Global Constitutionalism," in Falk, Johansen and Kim, eds., *Constitutional Foundations*, pp. 39-54 (p. 39).

12. George F. Kennan, "Diplomacy in the modern world," in John A. Vasquez, ed., *Classics of International Relations* (3. Ed., Upper Saddle River, NJ: Prentice Hall, 1996), pp. 28-31 (pp. 28-9).

13. The brand of 'deconstructivist' critical theory referred to here as neo-Marxian has to be distinguished from the paradigm of critical social theory as mentioned above. Major works in deconstructivist critical theory include James Der Derian, *Antidiplomacy. Spies, Terror, Speed, and War* (Oxford: Blackwell, 1992); James Der Derian and Michael J. Shapiro, eds., *International/Intertextual Relations. Postmodern Readings in World Politics* (Lexington, MA: Lexington Books, 1989); Michael J. Shapiro, *Reading the Postmodern Polity. Political Theory as Textual Practice* (Minneapolis, MN: University of Minnesota Press, 1992). Typical critical-deconstructivist statements also include Bradley S. Klein, "How the West was One: Representational Politics of NATO," *International Studies Quarterly* 34 (1990), pp. 311-25"; Timoty W. Luke, "Discourses of Disintegration, Texts of Transformation: Re-Reading Realism in the New World Order," *Alternatives* 18 (1993),

pp. 229-58 and Richard W. Mansbach, "The World Turned Upside Down," *Journal of East-Asian Affairs* 7 (1993), pp. 451-97.

14. Richard W. Mansbach, "The World Turned Upside Down," p. 483.

15. Cf. Robert J. Lieber, "Existential Realism After the Cold War," *Washington Quarterly* 16 (1993), No. 1, pp. 155-68; R. Harrison Wagner, "What was bipolarity?" *International Organization* 47 (1993), pp. 77-106 (pp. 77-9 and 103).

16. For the following figures, see *SIPRI Yearbook 1993* (Oxford: Oxford University Press, 1993), pp. 81-130; "Wars and Armed Conflict in 1993," graphics made up at the University of Leiden using data from the PIOOM database; Peter Wallensteen and Margareta Sollenberg, "After the Cold War: Emerging Patterns of Armed Conflict 1989-94," *Journal of Peace Research* 32 (1995), pp. 345-60.

17. See James E. Goodby, "Collective Security in Europe after the Cold War," *Journal of International Affairs* 46 (1993), pp. 299-321 (pp. 175-6); Kim R. Holmes, "New World Disorder: A Critique of the United Nations," *Journal of International Affairs* 46 (1993), pp. 323-40 (p. 324); Siedschlag, *Neorealismus*, pp. 231-2.

18. These distinctive features of general realist thought and methodology have, however, become somewhat blurred by the Waltzian enterprise to make realism a rigorous science, like for example economics, thus following the model of deductive reasoning and giving a number of well-defined, fixed principles and cause-effect assumptions prevalence over historical-hermeneutic and inductive cognitive styles.

19. See Lieber, "Existential Realism".

20. Cf. ibid., p. 155; see also Christopher Layne, "Kant or Cant. The Myth of Democratic Peace," *International Security* 19 (1994), No. 2, pp. 5-49 (p. 11).

21. Lieber, "Existential Realism," pp. 156-7.

22. See Barry R. Posen, "Security Dilemma and Ethnic Conflict," pp. 103-5.

23. Ibid., p. 103.

24. Goldmann, *Logic of Internationalism*.

25. Alexander Siedschlag, "Peaceful Settlement of Disputes and Conflict Management in Areas of ethno-national Tension," in Jörg Calließ and Christine M. Merkel, eds., *Peaceful Settlement of Conflicts as a Joint Task for International Organizations, Governments and Civil Society*. Vol. 1 (Rehburg-Loccum: Evangelische Akademie Loccum, 1995), pp. 35-56.

26. Cf. also Layne, "Kant or Cant," p. 11.

27. This becomes especially obvious in the debate about "new collective security" within a fully activated UN, see for example George W. Downs, ed., *Collective Security Beyond the Cold War* (Ann Arbor, MI: University of Michigan Press, 1994) and Thomas G. Weiss, ed., *Collective Security in a Changing World* (Boulder, CO: Rienner, 1993); see also Goodby, "Collective Security in Europe after the Cold War".

28. Hans J. Morgenthau and Kenneth W. Thompson, *Politics Among Nations. The Struggle for Power and Peace* (6. Ed., New York: Knopf, 1985), pp. 296-99.

29. Alan James, *Peacekeeping in International Politics* (Houndmills: Macmillan, 1990).

30. Rosemary Righter, *Utopia Lost. The United Nations and World Order* (New York: Twentieth Century Fund Press, 1995), p. 376.

31. Speech by the Secretary General of NATO Mr Manfred Wörner at the annual General Assembly of the International Press Institute. NATO Press Office, 10 May 1993, pp. 5-7.

32. The 40th General Assembly of the Atlantic Treaty Association, the Hague, the Netherlands. Address by Willy Claes, Secretary General of NATO. Friday, 28th October 1994.
33. MC 327, cited in Patricia Chilton et. al., *NATO, Peacekeeping, and the United Nations* (London: British American Security Information Council, 1994), p. 45.
34. MC 327, cited in ibid., p. 46.
35. Ibid.
36. The Clinton Administration's Policy on Reforming Multilateral Peace Operations. Washington, D.C., 4 May 1994 (= Presidential Decision Directive [PDD] 25), pp. 3 and 9.
37. John Mackinlay, "Improving Multifunctional Forces," *Survival* 36 (1994), No. 3, pp. 149-73, p. 152.
38. Sherard Cowper-Coles, "From Defence to Security: British Policy in Transition," *Survival* 36 (1994), No. 1, pp.142-61.
39. Bernard Bressy, "Trois *livres blancs* européens sur la défense," *Défense nationale* 50 (1994), No. 11, pp. 75-87 (p. 78).
40. Inis L. Claude, *Swords Into Plowshares. Problems and Progress of International Organization* (4. Ed., New York: McGraw-Hill, 1984), p. 265.
41. See already Marc Bentinck, *NATO's Out-of-Area Problem* (London: IISS, 1986) and for a newer treatment Bruce Scott, "NATO after Iraq: Out of Sector, or Out of Business?" *European Security* 2 (1993), pp. 227-43.
42. See Douglas Stuart and William Tow, *The Limits of Alliance. NATO Out-of-Area Problems Since 1949* (Baltimore, MD: Johns Hopkins University Press, 1990).
43. Bentinck, *Out of Area*, p. 6.
44. William Johnsen and Thomas-Durell Young, *Preparing for the NATO Summit: What are the Pivotal Issues?* (Carlisle, PA: U.S. Army War College, Strategic Studies Institute, 1993), pp. 1, 10 and 18.
45. Bentinck, *Out of Area*, p. 12.
46. Ibid., p. 9.
47. See George Stein, "The Euro-Corps and Future European Security Architecture," *European Security* 2 (1993), pp. 200-26 (pp. 218-9).

Chapter Four: The Regional Dimension - NATO's Institutional Adaptation

1. In the sense of constituting an *international regime* as defined by Stephen D. Krasner, "Structural causes and regime consequences: regimes as intervening variables," in Stephen D. Krasner, ed., *International Regimes* (Ithaca, NY: Cornell University Press, 1983), pp. 1-21 (p. 1).
2. See Bernard Bressy, "Trois *livres blancs* européens sur la défense," *Défense nationale* 50 (1994), No. 11, pp. 75-87 (p. 84).
3. See *Weißbuch 1994. Weißbuch zur Sicherheit der Bundesrepublik Deutschland und zur Lage und Zukunft der Bundeswehr* (Bonn: Ministry of Defense, 1994), para. 208 and 308.
4. Cf. Michael Brenner, "The Multilateral Moment," in Michael Brenner, ed., *Multilateralism and Western Strategy* (New York: Columbia University Press, 1995), pp. 1-41 (p. 8); John F. Duffield, "NATO's Functions after the Cold War," *Political Science Quarterly* 109 (1994/95), pp. 763-87 (p. 777); David G. Haglund, "Must NATO fail? Theories, myths, and policy dilemmas," *International Journal* 50 (1995), pp. 651-74 (p. 662).

5. Cf. Haglund, "Must NATO fail?", pp. 663-4 and 673-4; Steve Weber, "Does NATO have a future?" in Beverly Crawford, ed., *The Future of European Security* (Berkeley, CA: University of California Press, 1992), pp. 360-95 (p. 362-68).

6. Weber, "Does NATO have a future?", pp. 363-4; but cf. equivalent long-standing assumptions held by neorealist alliance theory as promoted by Glenn H. Synder, "The Security Dilemma in Alliance Politics," *World Politics* 36 (1984), pp. 461-95 (pp. 485 and 494-5).

7. Following Robert O. Keohane, *After Hegemony. Cooperation and Discord in the World Political Economy* (Princeton, NJ: Princeton University Press, 1984), p. 63; Robert O. Keohane, *International Institutions and State Power. Essays in International Relations Theory* (Boulder, CO: Westview, 1989), pp. 8 and 11.

8. Cf. William Wallace, "European-Atlantic Security Institutions: Current State and Future Prospects," *International Spectator* 29 (1994), No. 3, pp. 37-51 (p. 45).

9. Cf. Kenneth N. Waltz, "Reflections on Theory of International Politics: A Response to My Critics," in Robert O. Keohane, ed., *Neorealism and Its Critics* (New York: Columbia University Press, 1986), pp. 322-45 (p. 336).

10. See Simon Duke, *The New European Security Disorder* (New York: St. Martin's Press, 1993), p. 311. This last-named implicit dimension alone would have given enough reason for a sincere self-revision of the Alliance along with the beginning decomposition of the post-World War II world politics' bipolar texture, as has been pointed out by Wallace, "European-Atlantic Security Institutions," pp. 45-6, with the underlying aim being precisely to keep NATO's international-political "position" in the Waltzian sense.

11. London Declaration on a Transformed North Atlantic Alliance. Issued by the Heads of State and Government participating in the meeting of the North Atlantic Council in London on 5th-6th July 1990, para. 1.

12. Ibid., para. 2.

13. The Alliance's new Strategic Concept. Agreed by the Heads of State and Government participating in the meeting of the North Atlantic Council in Rome on 7th-8th November 1991, para. 20 and 43.

14. James B. Steinberg, *Overlapping Institutions, Underinsured Security: The Evolution of the Post-Cold War Security Order* (Santa Monica, CA: RAND, 1993), p. 6.

15. The Alliance's new Strategic Concept, para. 9.

16. This follows for example from the general assumptions about inter-state cooperative behavior made in Robert O. Keohane, *After Hegemony*, pp. 89-109.

17. Ibid., pp. 100-1.

18. See Robert O. Keohane, "Institutional Theory and the Realist Challenge after the Cold War," in David A. Baldwin, ed., *Neorealism and Neoliberalism. The Contemporary Debate* (New York: Columbia University Press, 1993), pp. 269-300 (p. 287).

19. Madrid Declaration on Euro-Atlantic Security and Cooperation. Issued by the Heads of State and Government participating in the meeting of the North Atlantic Council in Madrid on 8th July 1997 (NATO Press Communiqué M-1[97]81, 8 July 1997), para. 2-3.

20. The Alliance's new Strategic Concept, para. 15-6.

21. Alexander Moens, "The Formative Years of the New NATO: Diplomacy from London to Rome," in Alexander Moens and Christopher Anstis, eds., *Disconcerted Europe. The Search for a New Security Architecture* (Boulder, CO: Westview, 1994), pp. 24-47.

22. This national dimension is treated in further detail in ch. 5.

23. This concept has been developed by what could be called the German school of policy network analysis, see for example Fritz W. Scharpf, "Die Handlungsfähigkeit des Staates am Ende des zwanzigsten Jahrhunderts," *Politische Vierteljahresschrift* 32 (1991), pp. 621-34 (p. 630).

24. Ibid.

25. Ibid.

26. See Joseph M. Grieco, "State Interests and Institutional Rule Trajectories: A Neorealist Interpretation of the Maastricht Treaty and the European Economic and Monetary Union," in Benjamin Frankel, ed., *Realism. Restatement and Renewal* (London: Cass, 1996), pp. 261-301 (pp. 287-8).

27. Ibid., p. 287.

28. Ibid., p. 288.

29. The argument follows my *Die aktive Beteiligung Deutschlands and militärischen Aktionen zur Verwirklichung Kollektiver Sicherheit* (Frankfurt/M.: Peter Lang, 1995), pp. 158-9. See also Finn Laursen, "The Common Foreign and Security Policy of the European Union: Words or Deeds?" in Ingo Peters, ed., *New Security Challenges: The Adaptation of International Institutions. Reforming the UN, NATO, EU and CSCE Since 1989* (New York: St. Martin's Press, 1996), pp. 153-77.

30. On this concept, see Andrew Moravcsik, "Introduction. Integrating International and Domestic Theories of International Bargaining," in Peter B. Evans, Harold K. Jacobson and Robert D. Putnam, eds., *Double-Edged Diplomacy. International Bargaining and Domestic Politics* (Berkeley, CA: University of California Press, 1993), pp. 3-42 (pp. 31-2).

31. On these points, see Alexander Wendt, "The Agent-Structure Problem in International Relations Theory," *International Organization* 4 (1987), No. 3, pp. 335-70 (p. 364).

32. Ibid., p. 362.

33. Ibid., p. 364.

34. Cf. James G. March and Johan P. Olsen, *Rediscovering Institutions. The Organizational Basis of Politics* (New York: The Free Press, 1989), pp. 160-162.

35. Speech by the Secretary General of NATO Mr Manfred Wörner at the annual General Assembly of the International Press Institute. NATO Press Office, 10 May 1993, p. 3.

36. Ibid., p. 7.

37. Ibid., p. 7.

38. William Johnsen and Thomas-Durell Young, *Preparing for the NATO Summit: What are the Pivotal Issues?* (Carlisle, PA: U.S. Army War College, Strategic Studies Institute, 1993).

39. Cf. Declaration of the Heads of State and Government participating in the Meeting of the North Atlantic Council held at NATO Headquarters, Brussels, on 10-11 January 1994 (NATO Press Communiqué M-1[94]3, 11 January 1994), para. 1 and appendix.

40. Ibid., para. 7-9.

41. Peter Schmidt, *Germany, France and NATO* (Carlisle, PA: U.S. Army War College, Strategic Studies Institute, 1994), p. 14.

42. Ibid.

43. Rome Declaration on Peace and Cooperation. Issued by the Heads of State and Government participating in the meeting of the North Atlantic Council in Rome on 7th-8th November 1991 (NATO Press Communiqué S-1[91]86, 8 November 1991), para. 3.

44. Ibid., para. 6.

45. See Andrew M. Dorman and Adrian Treacher, *European Security. An Introduction to Security Issues in Post-Cold War Europe* (Aldershot: Dartmouth, 1995), pp. 43-73.

46. On the following, see Hugh De Santis, "Romancing NATO: Partnership for Peace and East European Stability," in Ted G. Carpenter, ed., *The Future of NATO* (London: Cass, 1995), pp. 61-81 (p. 63).

47. NATO Press Release M-DPC/NPG-2(95)117, para. 24.

48. See Ministerial Meeting of the North Atlantic Council in Berlin, 3 June 1996. Final Communiqué (NATO Press Communiqué M-NAC-1[96]63, 3 June 1996), para. 5-6.

49. See Declaration of the Heads of State and Government, para. 6.

50. See Charles Barry, "NATO's Combined Joint Task Forces in Theory and Practice," *Survival* 38 (1996), No. 1, pp. 81-97.

51. "After the NATO Summit: New structures and modalities for military cooperation," explanatory memorandum by Rafael Estrella for the North Atlantic Assembly (NAA, AL 205/DSC [94], 8 November 1994), pp. 16-7.

52. Stanley R. Sloan, ed., *NATO in the 1990s* (Washington, D.C.: Pergamon-Brassey's, 1989).

53. Ibid., p. 215.

54. Ibid., pp. 14-5.

55. Ibid., p. 17.

56. Ibid.

57. Ministerial Meeting of the North Atlantic Council in Sintra, Portugal. Final Communiqué, 29 May 1997 (NATO Press Communiqué M-NAC-1[97]65).

58. Gunther Hellmann and Reinhard Wolf, "Neorealism, Neoliberal Institutionalism, and the Future of NATO," *Security Studies* 3 (1993), pp. 3-43.

59. See Declaration of the Heads of State and Government, para. 12.

60. In the terminology of Waltz, "Reflections," p. 336.

61. See Kenneth N. Waltz, *Theory of International Politics* (New York: McGraw-Hill, 1979), p. 92.

62. Cf. ibid., p. 126.

63. See Kenneth N. Waltz, "The Emerging Structure of International Politics," *International Security* 18 (1993), No. 2, pp. 44-79 (p. 76); John J. Mearsheimer, "Back to the Future. Instability in Europe After the Cold War," *International Security* 15 (1990), No. 1, pp. 5-56 (p. 52).

64. On this, see Helen Milner, "International Theories of Cooperation Among Nations. Strengths and Weaknesses," *World Politics* 44 (1992), pp. 466-96 (pp. 473-4).

65. Robert O. Keohane, "The Analysis of International Regimes. Towards a European-American Research Programme," in Volker Rittberger, ed., *Regime Theory and International Relations* (Oxford: Clarendon, 1993), pp. 23-45 (pp. 39-40).

66. "The Western European Union in the 1990s: Searching for a Role," Strategic Outreach Conference Report, U.S. Army War College, Strategic Studies Institute, Carlisle, PA, 1993, p. 1.

67. Keohane, *International Institutions*, pp. 8-9 for instance expects a general conflict-ameliorating effect of a political condition of "complex interdependence" and a related reciprocity in international relations, oriented along growing common "conventions". This optimism is not only typical of the Keohane branch of neoliberalism but of the neoliberal paradigm in general. See related assumptions made by J. Martin Rochester, "The United Nations in a New World Order: Reviving the Theory and Practice of International Organi-

zation," in Charles W. Kegley, ed., *Controversies in International Relations Theory. Realism and the Neoliberal Challenge* (New York: St. Martin's Press, 1995), pp. 199-221 and Mark W. Zacher, "Toward a Theory of International Regimes," *Journal of International Affairs* 44 (1990), pp. 139-57.

68. Barry Buzan et. al., *The European Security Order Recast. Scenarios for the Post-Cold War World* (London: Pinter, 1990); Barry Buzan et. al., *Identity, Migration and the New Security Agenda in Europe* (New York: St. Martin's Press, 1993).

69. Ted Hopf, "Managing the Post-Soviet Security Space: A Continuing Demand for Behavioral Regimes," *Security Studies* 4 (1994/95), pp. 242-80.

70. Basic Document on the Euro-Atlantic Partnership Council (NATO Press Release M-NACC-EAPC-1[97]66, 30 May 1997), para. 3-4.

Chapter Five: The National Dimension - Individual vs. Common Goods

1. See, respectively, Charles W. Kegley and Gregory A. Raymond, *A Multipolar Peace? Great-Power Politics in the Twenty-first Century* (New York: St. Martin's Press, 1994); Richard A. Falk, Robert C. Johansen and Samuel S. Kim, eds., *The Constitutional Foundations of World Peace* (Albany, NY: State University of New York Press, 1993); Bradley S. Klein, "After Strategy: The Search for a Post-Modern Politics of Peace," *Alternatives* 13 (1988), pp. 293-318.

2. For a history of U.S. foreign and security policy since 1945, see Seyom Brown, *The Faces of Power. Constancy and Change in United States Foreign Policy from Truman to Clinton* (2. Ed., New York: Columbia University Press, 1994).

3. On the traditional tension between realpolitik and idealpolitk in U.S. foreign policy, see Hans J. Morgenthau, *Scientific Man vs. Power Politics* (Chicago: Chicago University Press, 1946), esp. pp. 5-10.

4. See *A National Security Strategy of Engagement and Enlargement* (Washington, D.C.: The White House, July 1994).

5. Robert A. Levine, "The United States," in Robert A. Levine, ed., *Transition and Turmoil in the Atlantic Alliance* (New York: Crane Russak, 1992), pp. 13-29 (p. 14).

6. Ibid., p. 15.

7. Article 4 reads: "The Parties will consult together whenever, in the opinion of any of them, the territorial integrity, political independence or security of any of the Parties is threatened."

8. For this concept, see Paul A. Chilton, *Security Metaphors. Cold War Discourse from Containment to Common House* (New York: Peter Lang, 1996).

9. Ted G. Carpenter, *Beyond NATO. Staying out of Europe's Wars* (Washington, D.C.: CATO Institute, 1994), p. 4.

10. See *A National Security Strategy*, pp. 21-7.

11. The Clinton Administration's Policy on Reforming Multilateral Peace Operations, Washington, D.C., 4 May 1994 (= Presidential Decision Directive [PDD] 25), p. 1.

12. Ibid., pp. 1 and 3.

13. See *A National Security Strategy*, p. 13.

14. Ibid.

15. Ibid., p. 10.

16. The Clinton Administration's Policy on Reforming Multilateral Peace Operations, p. 9.
17. John Mackinlay, "Improving Multifunctional Forces," *Survival* 36 (1994), No. 3, pp. 149-73 (p. 155).
18. Ibid., p. 156.
19. See Morgenthau, *Scientific Man*, esp. pp. 5-10.
20. See Paul Seabury, *Power, Freedom and Diplomacy* (New York: Random House, 1963).
21. Stanley Kober, "Idealpolitik," *Foreign Policy*, No. 79 (1990), pp. 3-24 (p. 22).
22. Joseph S. Nye, "American power and a post-cold war world," in *Facing the Future: American Strategy in the 1990s* (Lanham, ML: Aspen Institute, 1991), pp. 33-54.
23. Robert S. Chase, Emily B. Hill and Paul Kennedy, "Pivotal states and U.S. strategy," *Foreign Affairs* 75 (1996), pp. 33-51.
24. See the critics by Charles W. Maynes, "A workable Clinton doctrine," *Foreign Policy*, No. 93 (1993/94), pp. 3-20 and Malcolm Wallop, "America needs a post-containment doctrine," *Orbis* 37 (1993), pp. 187-203.
25. Sherard Cowper-Coles, "From Defence to Security: British Policy in Transition," *Survival* 36 (1994), No. 1, pp. 142-61 (pp. 152-3).
26. Ibid., p. 147.
27. See ibid. and Michael Clarke and Philip Sabin, eds., *British Defence Choices for the Twenty-first Century* (London: Brassey's, 1993).
28. Cowper-Coles, "From Defence to Security," p. 147.
29. *Statement on the Defence Estimates 1995. Stable Forces in a Strong Britain* (London: HMSO, 1995).
30. Ibid., para. 302-29.
31. Ibid., para. 331-4.
32. Ibid., para. 335-64 (quotation in para. 336).
33. Cf. David Greenwood, "United Kingdom," in Douglas J. Murray and Paul R. Viotti, eds., *The Defense Policies of Nations* (3. Ed., Baltimore, MD: Johns Hopkins University Press, 1994), pp. 278-304 (p. 281).
34. See Bernard Bressy, "Trois *livres blancs* européens sur la défense," *Défense nationale* 50 (1994), No., 11, pp. 75-87 (p.84).
35. See Robbin F. Laird, "The West Europeans and peace-keeping," in James Cooney et. al., eds., *Deutsch-Amerikanische Beziehungen, Jahrbuch 2* (Frankfurt/M.: Campus, 1994), pp. 107-27 (p. 109).
36. Greenwood, "United Kingdom," pp. 280-1.
37. *Defence Estimates 1995*, para. 201-3 and 207.
38. See Mackinlay, "Multifunctional Forces," p. 155.
39. Ibid., p. 156.
40. Ibid.
41. Ibid., p. 113.
42. Ibid., pp. 118-9.
43. For a comprehensive history of French foreign affairs with a special focus on military and defense policy, see Jean Doise and Maurice Vaïsse, *Politique étrangère de la France. Diplomatie et outil militaire 1871-1991* (Paris: Seuil, 1992).
44. Cf. Uwe Nerlich, "Neue Sicherheitsfunktionen der NATO," in *Europa-Archiv* 48 (1993), pp. 663-72 (pp. 664-5).

45. See William Johnsen and Thomas-Durell Young, *French Policy Toward NATO: Enhanced Selectivity, Vice Rapprochement* (Carlisle, PA: U.S. Army War College, Strategic Studies Institute, 1994), p. 9.

46. David S. Yost, "France and the Gulf War of 1990-1991. Political-military lessons learned," *Journal of Strategic Studies* 16 (1993), pp. 339-74.

47. Cf. ibid., p. 354.

48. See Ministerial Meeting of the North Atlantic Council in Berlin, 3 June 1996. Final Communiqué (NATO Press Communiqué M-NAC-1[96]63, 3 June 1996), esp. para. 7-8.

49. See also the assessment in Johnsen and Young, *French Policy*.

50. Cited in Bressy, "Trois *livres blancs*," p. 78.

51. See Alexander Siedschlag, "Deutsche Außenpolitik im Dilemma der doppelten Normilität," *Jahrbuch für Politik* 5 (1995), pp. 297-318.

52. On this still virulent fear of 'the Germans', see Bruce N. Goldberger, "Why Europe should not fear the Germans," *German Politics* 2 (1993), pp. 288-310.

53. See Robert G. Livingston, "United Germany: bigger and better," *Foreign Policy*, no. 85 (1992), pp. 157-74.

54. See Uwe Nerlich, "Deutsche Sicherheitspolitik und Konflikte außerhalb des NATO-Gebiets," *Europa-Archiv* 46 (1991), pp. 303-10.

55. See Jeffrey T. Bergner, "Unified Germany: a great power with many options," in Gary L. Geipel, ed., *Germany in a New Era* (Indianapolis, ID: Hudson Institute, 1993), pp. 183-98.

56. See Ronald D. Asmus, "The future of German strategic thinking," in Geipel, ed., *Germany in a New Era*, pp. 137-81 (pp. 169-76).

57. See Anne-Marie Le Gloannec, "The implications of German unification for Western Europe," in Paul B. Stares, ed., *The New Germany and the New Europe* (Washington, D.C.: Brookings, 1992), pp. 251-78 (pp. 259-60).

58. See Thomas Kielinger and Max Otte, "Germany: the pressured power," *Foreign Policy*, no. 91 (1993), pp. 44-62.

59. See Clay Clemens, "Opportunity or obligation? Redefining Germany's military role outside of NATO," *Armed Forces and Society* 19 (1993), pp. 231-51.

60. *Weißbuch 1994. Weißbuch zur Sicherheit der Bundesrepublik Deutschland und zur Lage und Zukunft der Bundeswehr* (Bonn: Ministry of Defense, 1994), para. 317.

61. Cf. Anpassung der Streitkräftestrukturen, der Territorialen Wehrverwaltung und der Stationierung. Bonn, Ministry of Defense, October 1995; "Die Bundeswehr der Zukunft. Bundeswehrplan 94 vom 15. Dezember 1992," *EXTRA. Brief zur Truppeninformation*, No. 2/1992, p. 3.

62. "Die Bundeswehr der Zukunft," p. 3.

63. Julian Lider, *Origins and Development of West German Military Thought*. Vol. 2: *1966-1988* (Aldershot: Gower, 1988), pp. 541-2 and 544.

64. Wolfram F. Hanrieder, *West German Policy 1949-1963. International Pressure and Domestic Response* (Stanford, CA: Stanford University Press, 1967).

65. Wolfgang F. Schlör, *German Security Policy. An Examination of the Trends in German Security Policy in a New European and Global Context* (London: IISS, 1993), p. 6.

66. In part, see Julian Lider, *Origins and Development of West German Military Thought*. Vol. 1: *1949-1966* (Aldershot: Gower, 1986), pp. 255-96 and 319-41.

67. Klaus Naumann, *Die Bundeswehr in einer Welt im Umbruch* (Berlin: Siedler, 1994), p. 84.

68. For a recent account of this legacy from the Bundeswehr's tradition as an 'Alliance army' of only minimal national operational command capabilities so to minimize international fears of a reviving German militarism and to reflect its exclusive role as a territorial 'blocking' force against a large ground attack, see Thomas-Durell Young, "German national command structures after unification: A new German general staff?" *Armed Forces and Society* 22 (1996), pp. 379-417.

69. See Lothar Gutjahr, *German Foreign and Defence Policy After Unification* (London: Pinter, 1994), pp. 80-3; Stephen F. Szabo, *The Changing Politics of German Security* (New York: St. Martin's Press, 1990), pp. 125-34.

70. Timothy G. Ash, "Germany's choice," *Foreign Affairs* 73 (1994), No. 4, pp. 65-81 (p. 79).

71. Cf. the assessment by George Stein, "The Euro-Corps and Future European Security Architecture," *European Security* 2 (1993), pp. 200-26, p. 223.

72. Young, "German national command structures," p. 396.

73. *Weißbuch 1994*, para. 463.

74. Ressortkonzept zur Anpassung der Streitkräftestrukturen, der Territorialen Wehrverwaltung und der Stationierung. Bonn, Ministry of Defense, 15 March 1995.

75. "Die Bundeswehr der Zukunft," p. 2.

76. For some attempts to localize the U.S. in the new international setting and to derive corresponding recommendations for security policy, see for example John L. Gaddis, "Towards the post-cold war world," *Foreign Affairs* 70 (1991), pp. 102-116; William G. Hyland, "America's new course," *Foreign Affairs* 69 (1990), pp. 1-2; Charles William Maynes, "America without cold war," *Foreign Policy*, No. 78 (1990), pp. 3-25.

77. As suggested by David Campbell, *Writing Security: United States Foreign Policy and the Politics of Identity* (Minneapolis, MN: University of Minnesota Press, 1992), pp. 1-12 and 18.

78. Ibid.

79. Cited in: "Towards a Security Strategy for Europe and NATO," draft General Report by Mr. Jan Petersen, North Atlantic Assembly, Political Committee, October 1995 (AM 293/PC [95] 10), Introduction.

80. David G. Haglund, "Must NATO fail? Theories, myths, and policy dilemmas," *International Journal* 50 (1995), pp. 651-74, pp. 663-4.

81. "Towards a Security Strategy for Europe and NATO," para. 2.

82. "Study on NATO Enlargement," Brussels, September 1995.

83. See Glenn H. Snyder, "The Security Dilemma in Alliance Politics," *World Politics* 36 (1984), pp. 461-95 and Glenn H. Snyder, "Alliance Theory: A Neorealist First Cut," *Journal of International Affairs* 44 (1990), pp. 103-23.

84. "Towards a Security Strategy for Europe and NATO," para. 9.

85. David Carment, "NATO and the International Politics of Ethnic Conflict: Perspectives on Theory and Policy," *Contemporary Security Policy* 16 (1995), pp. 347-379 (p. 373).

86. Ibid.

87. Ibid.

88. Franz-Josef Meiers, *NATO's Peacekeeping Dilemma* (Bonn: Europa Union Verlag, 1996), p. 24.

89. Ibid., pp. 24-5.

90. Ibid., p. 5.

91. Ibid., pp. 17-23.
92. NATO's core security functions in the new Europe. North Atlantic Council meeting in Ministerial Session in Copenhagen on 6th and 7th June 1991 (NATO Press Communiqué M-1[91]44), para. 2-4.
93. See David Last and David B. Carment, "Conflict prevention and internal conflict," summary of a workshop held at Carleton University, Ontario, 8 March 1995.
94. See Pauline Neville-Jones, "Dayton, IFOR and Alliance Relations in Bosnia," *Survival* 38 (1996), No. 4, pp. 45-65 (pp. 54-59).
95. See "Towards a Security Strategy for Europe and NATO," para. 21.
96. Ministerial Meeting of the North Atlantic Council in Berlin, 3 June 1996, para. 7.

Chapter Six: Alliance Engagement under the Post-strategic Condition

1. See Michael Brenner, "The Multilateral Moment," in Michael Brenner, ed., *Multilateralism and Western Strategy* (New York: Columbia University Press, 1995), pp. 1-41; Charles W. Kegley and Gregory A. Raymond, *A Multipolar Peace? Great-Power Politics in the Twenty-first Century* (New York: St. Martin's Press, 1994); John G. Ruggie, ed., *Multilateralism Matters. The Theory and Praxis of an Institutional Form* (New York: Columbia University Press, 1993).
2. "A Future Security Agenda for Europe," report of the Independent Working Group established by the Stockholm International Peace Research Institute, 1996, p. 5.
3. See Alexis Seydoux and Jérôme Paolini, "From Interblocking to Institutional Evolutionism," in European Strategy Group, ed., *Challenges and Responses to Future European Security: British, French and German Perspectives* (n.p., 1993), pp. 171-202.
4. See Peter Schmidt, "The Evolution of European Security Structures: Master Plan or Trial and Error?" in David G. Haglund, ed., *From Euphoria to Hysteria. Western European Security After the Cold War* (Boulder, CO: Westview, 1993), pp. 145-66.
5. Cf. Alexis Seydoux and Jérôme Paolini, "From Interblocking to Institutional Evolutionism," p. 199.
6. A first step has been done with the development of MC 327, see ch. 3.3.
7. See Paul Bracken and Stuart E. Johnson, "Beyond NATO: Complementary militaries," *Orbis* 37 (1993), pp. 205-21.
8. See John Mackinlay, "Improving Multifunctional Forces," *Survival* 36 (1994), No. 3, pp. 149-73 (p. 167).
9. See especially the findings presented in K. M. de Silva and R. J. May, eds., *The Internationalization of Ethnic Conflict* (London: Pinter, 1991) and Stephen Ryan, *Ethnic Conflict and International Relations* (Aldershot: Dartmouth, 1990).
10. See Ryan, *Ethnic Conflict*, pp. 56-7.
11. Bradley S. Klein, "How the West was One: Representational Politics of NATO," *International Studies Quarterly* 34 (1990), pp. 311-25.

Chapter Seven: Conclusion and Outlook

1. Cf. Peter Katzenstein, ed., *The Culture of National Security* (New York: Columbia University Press, 1996).

2. Kenneth N. Waltz, *Theory of International Politics* (New York: McGraw-Hill, 1979), pp. 79-101.

3. In the terminology proposed by Patrick Morgan, "Multilateralism and Security: Prospects in Europe," in John G. Ruggie, ed., *Multilateralism Matters. The Theory and Praxis of an Institutional Form* (New York: Columbia University Press, 1993), pp. 327-64 (p. 346).

4. Nicholas J. Rengger, "No longer 'A Tournament of Distinctive Knights'? Systemic Transition and the Priority of International Order," in Mike Bowker and Richard Brown, eds., *From War to Collapse: Theory and World Politics in the 1980s* (Cambridge: Cambridge University Press, 1993), pp. 145-74.

5. Paul D. Miller, *Retaining Alliance Relevancy. NATO and the Combined Joint Task Force Concept* (Cambridge, MA: Institute for Foreign Policy Analysis, 1994).

Chronology: Hallmarks of NATO's Adaptation, 1990-1997

1990

6 July — NATO Heads of State and Government meeting in London publish the "London Declaration on a Transformed North Atlantic Alliance". The Declaration announces that "this Alliance must and will adapt." NATO is moving toward a new collective-defense concept, nuclear weapons becoming weapons of last resort. Its approach is, whereas retaining the primacy of collective self-defense, to sincerely review and revise the formulation of this common defense. Accordingly, the Alliance's integrated force structure and strategy is announced to change to fielding smaller and restructured active forces. These forces will be highly mobile and versatile so that Allied leaders will have maximum flexibility in deciding how to respond to a crisis. NATO will rely increasingly on multinational corps, made up of combined national units. The Declaration also outlines several possible forms of cooperation with the Central and Eastern European Countries, in political as well as military affairs, including the establishment of regular diplomatic liaison.

1991

6-7 June — NATO Foreign Ministers meeting in Copenhagen declare Europe's division overcome, opening up an era of common security for all European countries. Their common declaration underlines NATO's support for rendering the CSCE more effective and for the process of West European integration, as well as the envisaged Common Foreign and Security Policy. Four functions are seen central to NATO: 1. Providing the fundament for a security framework in Europe in which no nation may intimidate or coerce another; 2. Providing for a transatlantic forum for coordination and consultation between the Allies; 3. Maintaining dissuasion and defense against any aggression that is directed against a member state's territory; 4. Preserving a strategic balance in Europe.

7-8 November — Summit Meeting of the North Atlantic Council in Rome. "The Alliance's new Strategic Concept" is published, centering on dialogue, co-operation, a "broad approach to security", diplomatic liaison with the former Warsaw Pact Countries (whose dissolution was announced in April) and turning against a generalized enemy. The new Strategic Concept does not give up the traditional core functions of the Alliance but reaffirms them, at the same time acknowledging the need for far-reaching institutional changes exactly because of the continuance of its principle rationale. The Meeting also coins the phrase of "interlocking institutions" in the field of European security, with NATO envisaged to become the leading one.

11-13 December	Ministerial Meeting of the Euro Group and the countries participating in the newly established North Atlantic Cooperation Council (NACC), declaring that a collective approach to security remains essential and the deepened West European integration will strengthen that approach. The Meeting acknowledges that a broad approach to security also means to improve political and economic cooperation with the Central and Eastern European counties. With a view to the Yugoslav contingency, it is also underlines that war in Europe has become possible again.

1992

21 May	First formal meeting of the North Atlantic Council with the Council of the Western European Union, meaning reciprocal institutional recognition between NATO and WEU.
19 June	Petersberg Declaration of the Western European Union (WEU). The Declaration formally opens the door to autonomous West European military actions beyond the NATO framework, reaching from blue-helmet peace-keeping to collective defense. This marks the beginning of an interim period of institutional duplication in European security structures, rendering the concept of interlocking institutions one of interblocking ones.
18 December	NACC meeting, leading to a joint declaration of the participating countries' common will to support UN and CSCE operations.

1993

21 January	France and Germany sign an agreement with NATO about making the Eurocorps answerable to the Alliance. This is a new stage in relations between France and the Alliance's military structure as well as in shaping an operational European pillar.
12 April	Start of the NATO operation to enforce the no-fly zone over Bosnia, in implementation of UN Security Council Resolution 816. This is the Alliance's first military operation since its existence.
5 August	Draft of MC 327, entitled "NATO Military Planning for Peace Support Operations". French resistance prevented it from being agreed by the North Atlantic Council, but it came to be used within the integrated military structure. In MC 327, NATO declares itself in principle prepared to cooperate with the UN but underscores that NATO decisions will remain NATO decisions and no command and control authorities shall be transferred to the UN. Participation in peace support operations will remain subject to national decision and the Alliance intends to use its existing command structure to the greatest extend possible, with the

details to be determined on a case by case basis. MC 327 does not specify any responsibility to report to the UN on the part of NATO force commanders, the North Atlantic Council or the Defense Planning Committee. The commander of a NATO-supported UN force will normally be an Alliance flag or general officer, serving in an appropriate position in the integrated military structure.

1994

10-11 January	Brussels Summit of NATO Heads of State and Government. Partnership for Peace (PfP) is launched and the concept of Combined Joint Task Forces (CJTF) endorsed. The Alliance is officially declared open to new members. The Summit of Brussels also brought a significant step towards revising the concept of the Alliance's institutional adaptation from an at first seemingly envisaged catch-all approach to a more promising strategy of functional restraint.
29 September	For the first time in 28 years, the French Minister of Defense attends a NATO Defense Ministers' Meeting.

1995

27 September	The Study on NATO Enlargement is published.
5-6 December	At NATO's Foreign Ministers' Meeting in Brussels, French Foreign Minister de Charette announces his countries' return into the non-integrated military committees of the Alliance.
14 December	Agreement about the Dayton Peace Accord for Bosnia. NATO will take command over the Implementation Force (IFOR).
20 December	Transfer of authority from UNPROFOR to NATO. The IFOR mission begins. 60.000 troops from 26 nations, including 17 non-NATO countries, participate in the mission.

1996

3 June	NATO Council Ministerial Meeting in Berlin. It marks a decisive turning point, officially giving up NATO's claim to an ever-leading role in the interplay of European security institutions, turning to the new principle of *interacting institutions* - namely a coordinated interplay of the different European security institutions that does not rest upon one lead-institution but rather on the idea of general common regulations for well-defined functional sharing. So, after a time of functional diffusion and catch-all security rhetorics, the Berlin Ministerial Meeting yields a

	clear reorientation to an Alliance strategy of functional specificity, centering on three main objectives: ensuring the Alliance's military effectiveness so that it is able to perform its traditional mission of collective defense, and through flexible and agreed procedures to undertake new roles in changing circumstances; preserving the transatlantic link; developing the European Security and Defense Identity *within* the Alliance, taking full advantage of the CJTF concept.
10 December	Agreement about a Stabilization Force (SFOR) for Bosnia, as a follow-up to IFOR and also commanded by NATO.

1997

27 May	NATO concludes a Founding Act with Russia, with a permanent NATO-Russia Council established.
29 May	NATO initials a charter with Ukraine, with a NATO-Ukraine Commission to be installed.
29-30 June	NATO's Foreign Ministers meeting at Sintra prepare the 'Enlargement Summit' of Madrid and decide to replace NACC by the newly founded Euro-Atlantic Partnership Council (EAPC).
8-9 July	At their Madrid Summit Meeting, NATO Heads of State and Government set a milestone in the process of the Alliance's institutional adaptation. Formally inviting the Czech Republic, Hungary and Poland to start negotiations about joining the North Atlantic Treaty, they open a second track in the NATO's adapting process, the one of 'external' adaptation (in contrast to the - still ongoing and continuing - process of 'internal' political and military adaptation as rung in by the London Declaration of July 1990). They reaffirm that NATO remains open to new members under Article 10 of the North Atlantic Treaty and that the Alliance will continue to welcome new members in a position to further the principles of the Treaty and contribute to security in the Euro-Atlantic area.

Bibliography

Documents and Sources

A National Security Strategy of Engagement and Enlargement. Washington, D.C.: The White House, July 1994.

"After the NATO Summit: New structures and modalities for military cooperation," explanatory memorandum by Rafael Estrella for the North Atlantic Assembly, 8 November 1994 (NAA, AL 205/DSC [94]).

Anpassung der Streitkräftestrukturen, der Territorialen Wehrverwaltung und der Stationierung. Bonn, Ministry of Defense, October 1995.

Basic Document on the Euro-Atlantic Partnership Council (NATO Press Release M-NACC-EAPC-1[97]66, 30 May 1997).

Declaration of the Heads of State and Government participating in the Meeting of the North Atlantic Council held at NATO Headquarters, Brussels, on 10-11 January 1994 (NATO Press Communiqué M-1[94]3, 11 January 1994).

"Die Bundeswehr der Zukunft. Bundeswehrplan 94 vom 15. Dezember 1992," *EXTRA. Brief zur Truppeninformation,* No. 2/1992.

London Declaration on a Transformed North Atlantic Alliance. Issued by the Heads of State and Government participating in the meeting of the North Atlantic Council in London on 5th-6th July 1990.

Madrid Declaration on Euro-Atlantic Security and Cooperation. Issued by the Heads of State and Government participating in the meeting of the North Atlantic Council in Madrid on 8th July 1997 (NATO Press Communiqué M-1[97]81, 8 July 1997).

Ministerial Meeting of the North Atlantic Council in Berlin, 3 June 1996. Final Communiqué (NATO Press Communiqué M-NAC-1[96]63, *3* June 1996).

Ministerial Meeting of the North Atlantic Council in Sintra, Portugal. Final Communiqué, 29 May 1997 (NATO Press Communiqué M-NAC-1[97]65).

NATO Press Release M-DPC/NPG-2(95)117.

NATO's core security functions in the new Europe. North Atlantic Council meeting in Ministerial Session in Copenhagen on 6th and 7th June 1991 (NATO Press Communiqué M-1[91]44).

Ressortkonzept zur Anpassung der Streitkräftestrukturen, der Territorialen Wehrverwaltung und der Stationierung. Bonn, Ministry of Defense, 15 March 1995.

Rome Declaration on Peace and Cooperation. Issued by the Heads of State and Government participating in the meeting of the North Atlantic Council in Rome on 7th-8th November 1991 (NATO Press Communiqué S-1[91]86, 8 November 1991).

SIPRI Yearbook 1993. Oxford: Oxford University Press, 1993.

Speech by the Secretary General of NATO Mr Manfred Wörner at the annual General Assembly of the International Press Institute. NATO Press Office, 10 May 1993.

Statement on the Defence Estimates 1995. Stable Forces in a Strong Britain. London: HMSO, 1995.

"Study on NATO Enlargement," Brussels, September 1995.

The 40th General Assembly of the Atlantic Treaty Association, the Hague, the Netherlands. Address by Willy Claes, Secretary General of NATO. Friday, 28 October 1994.

The Alliance's new Strategic Concept. Agreed by the Heads of State and Government participating in the meeting of the North Atlantic Council in Rome on 7th-8th November 1991.

The Clinton Administration's Policy on Reforming Multilateral Peace Operations. Washington, D.C., 4 May 1994 (= Presidential Decision Directive [PDD] 25).

"Towards a Security Strategy for Europe and NATO," draft General Report by Mr. Jan Petersen, North Atlantic Assembly, Political Committee, October 1995 (AM 293/PC [95]10).

"Wars and Armed Conflict in 1993," graphics made up at the University of Leiden using data from the PIOOM database.

Weißbuch 1994. Weißbuch zur Sicherheit der Bundesrepublik Deutschland und zur Lage und Zukunft der Bundeswehr. Bonn: Ministry of Defense, 1994.

Literature

"A Future Security Agenda for Europe," report of the Independent Working Group established by the Stockholm International Peace Research Institute, 1996.

Alker, Hayward. *Rediscoveries and Reformulations. Humanistic Methodologies for International Studies.* Cambridge: Cambridge University Press, 1996.

Ash, Timothy G. "Germany's choice," *Foreign Affairs* 73 (1994), No. 4, pp. 65-81.

Asmus, Ronald D. "The future of German strategic thinking," pp. 137-81 in Gary L. Geipel, ed., *Germany in a New Era.* Indianapolis, ID: Hudson Institute, 1993.

Baldwin, David A., ed. *Neorealism and Neoliberalism. The Contemporary Debate.* New York: Columbia University Press, 1993.

Barry, Charles. "NATO's Combined Joint Task Forces in Theory and Practice," *Survival* 38 (1996), No. 1, pp. 81-97.

Bentinck, Marc. *NATO's Out-of-Area Problem.* London: IISS, 1986.

Bergner, Jeffrey T. "Unified Germany: a great power with many options," pp. 183-98 in Gary L. Geipel, ed., *Germany in a New Era.* Indianapolis, ID: Hudson Institute, 1993.

Bonvicini, Gianni, et. al., eds. *A Renewed Partnership for Europe.* Baden-Baden: Nomos, 1995/96.

Booth, Ken, and Nicholas Wheeler. "Contending philosophies about security in Europe," pp. 3-36 in Colin McInnes, ed., *Security and Strategy in the New Europe.* London: Routledge, 1992.

Bowker, Mike, and Richard Brown, eds. *From War to Collapse: Theory and World Politics in the 1980s.* Cambridge: Cambridge University Press, 1993.

Bracken, Paul, and Stuart E. Johnson. "Beyond NATO: Complementary militaries," *Orbis* 37 (1993), pp. 205-21.

Brenner, Michael. "The Multilateral Moment," pp. 1-41 in Michael Brenner, ed., *Multilateralism and Western Strategy.* New York: Columbia University Press, 1995.

Bressy, Bernard. "Trois *livres blancs* européens sur la défense," *Défense nationale* 50 (1994), No. 11, pp. 75-87.

Brown, Seyom. *The Faces of Power. Constancy and Change in United States Foreign Policy from Truman to Clinton.* 2. Ed. New York: Columbia University Press, 1994.

Burchill, Scott, and Andrew Linklater. *Theories of International Relations.* Houndmills: Macmillan, 1996.

Buzan, Barry, Charles Jones, and Richard Little. *The Logic of Anarchy. Neorealism to Structural Realism.* New York: Columbia University Press, 1993.

Buzan, Barry, et. al. *The European Security Order Recast. Scenarios for the Post-Cold War Era.* London: Pinter, 1990.

——. *Identity, Migration and the New Security Agenda in Europe.* New York: St. Martin's Press, 1993.

Campbell, David. *Writing Security: United States Foreign Policy and the Politics of Identity.* Minneapolis, MN: University of Minnesota Press, 1992.

Caporaso, James A. "International relations theory and multilateralism: the search for foundations," *International Organization* 46 (1992), pp. 599-632.

Carey, Roger, and Trevor C. Salmon, eds. *International Security in the Modern World.* New York: St. Martin's Press, 1992.

Carment, David. "NATO and the International Politics of Ethnic Conflict: Perspectives on Theory and Policy," *Contemporary Security Policy* 16 (1995), pp. 347-79.

Carpenter, Ted G. *Beyond NATO. Staying out of Europe's Wars.* Washington, D.C.: CATO Institute, 1994.

Carpenter, Ted G., ed. *The Future of NATO.* London: Cass, 1995.

Chase, Robert S., Emily B. Hill, and Paul Kennedy. "Pivotal states and U.S. strategy," *Foreign Affairs* 75 (1996), pp. 33-51.

Chilton, Patricia, et. al. *NATO, Peacekeeping, and the United Nations.* London: British American Security Information Council, 1994.

Chilton, Paul A. *Security Metaphors. Cold War Discourse from Containment to Common House.* New York: Peter Lang, 1996.

Clarke, Michael, and Philip Sabin, eds. *British Defence Choices for the Twenty-first Century.* London: Brassey's, 1993.

Claude, Inis L. *Swords Into Plowshares. Problems and Progress of International Organization.* 4. Ed. New York: McGraw-Hill, 1984.

Clemens, Clay. "Opportunity or obligation? Redefining Germany's military role outside of NATO," *Armed Forces and Society* 19 (1993), pp. 231-51.

Cornish, Paul. "European security: the end of architecture and the new NATO," *International Affairs* (London) 72 (1996), pp. 751-69.

Cowper-Coles, Sherard. "From Defence to Security: British Policy in Transition," *Survival* 36 (1994), No. 1, pp.142-61.

Crawford, Neta C. "Once and Future Security Studies," *Security Studies* 1 (1991), pp. 283-316.

Czempiel, Ernst-Otto, and James N. Rosenau, eds. *Global Changes and Theoretical Challenges. Approaches to World Politics for the 1990s.* Lexington, MA: Lexington Books, 1989.

Der Derian, James. *Antidiplomacy. Spies, Terror, Speed, and War.* Oxford: Blackwell, 1992.

Der Derian, James, and Michael J. Shapiro, eds. *International/Intertextual Relations. Postmodern Readings in World Politics.* Lexington, MA: Lexington Books, 1989.

De Santis, Hugh. "Romancing NATO: Partnership for Peace and East European Stability," pp. 61-81 in Ted G. Carpenter, ed., *The Future of NATO.* London: Cass, 1995.

De Silva, K. M., and R. J. May, eds. *The Internationalization of Ethnic Conflict.* London: Pinter, 1991.

Doise, Jean, and Maurice Vaïsse. *Politique étrangère de la France. Diplomatie et outil militaire 1871-1991.* Paris: Seuil, 1992.

Dorman, Andrew M., and Adrian Treacher. *European Security. An Introduction to Security Issues in Post-Cold War Europe.* Aldershot: Dartmouth, 1995.

Downs, George W., ed. *Collective Security Beyond the Cold War.* Ann Arbor, MI: University of Michigan Press, 1994.

Duffield, John F. "NATO's functions after the Cold War," *Political Science Quarterly* 109 (1994/95), pp. 763-87.

Duke, Simon. *The New European Security Disorder.* New York: St. Martin's Press, 1993.

Evans, Peter B., Harold K. Jacobson, and Robert D. Putnam, eds. *Double-Edged Diplomacy. International Bargaining and Domestic Politics.* Berkeley, CA: University of California Press, 1993.

Falk, Richard A., Robert C. Johansen, and Samuel S. Kim, eds. *The Constitutional Foundations of World Peace.* Albany, NJ: State University of New York Press, 1993.

Frankel, Benjamin, ed. *Realism. Restatement and Renewal.* London: Cass, 1996.

Gaddis, John L. "Towards the post-cold war world," *Foreign Affairs* 70 (1991), pp. 102-16.

George, Alexander L. *Bridging the Gap. Theory and Practice in Foreign Policy.* Washington, D.C.: U.S. Institute of Peace, 1993.

Glaser, Charles L. "Why NATO is Still Best. Future Security Arrangements for Europe," *International Security* 18 (1993), No. 1, pp. 5-50.

Goldberger, Bruce N. "Why Europe should not fear the Germans," *German Politics* 2 (1993), pp. 288-310.

Goldmann, Kjell. *The Logic of Internationalism. Coercion and Accommodation.* London: Routledge, 1994.

Goldstein, Walter, ed. *Security in Europe: The Role of NATO After the Cold War.* London: Brassey's, 1994.

Goodby, James E. "Collective Security in Europe after the Cold War," *Journal of International Affairs* 46 (1993), pp. 299-321.

Gordon, Philip H., ed. *NATO's Transformation. The Changing Shape of the Atlantic Alliance.* Oxford: Rowman and Littlefield, 1997.

Grant, Robert P. "France's new relationship with NATO," *Survival* 38 (1996), No. 1, pp. 58-80.

Greenwood, David. "United Kingdom," pp. 278-304 in Douglas J. Murray and Paul R. Viotti, eds., *The Defense Policies of Nations.* 3. Ed. Baltimore, MD: Johns Hopkins University Press, 1994.

Grendstad, Gunnar, and Per Selle. "Cultural theory and the new institutionalism," *Journal of Theoretical Politics* 7 (1995), pp. 5-27.

Grieco, Joseph M. "Anarchy and the limits of cooperation: a realist critique of the newest liberal institutionalism," pp. 116-40 in David A. Baldwin, ed. *Neorealism and Neoliberalism: The Contemporary Debate.* New York: Columbia University Press, 1993.

———. "State Interests and Institutional Rule Trajectories: A Neorealist Interpretation of the Maastricht Treaty and the European Economic and Monetary Union," pp. 261-301 in Benjamin Frankel, ed., *Realism. Restatement and Renewal.* London: Cass, 1996.

Gutjahr, Lothar. *German Foreign and Defence Policy After Unification.* London: Pinter, 1994.

Haftendorn, Helga. "The Security Puzzle: Theory-Building and Discipline-Building in International Security," *International Studies Quarterly* 35 (1991), pp. 3-17.

Haglund, David G. "Must NATO fail? Theories, myths, and policy dilemmas," *International Journal* 50 (1995), pp. 651-74.

Halliday, Fred. *Rethinking International Relations*. Houndmills: Macmillan, 1994.
Hanrieder, Wolfram F. *West German Policy 1949-1963. International Pressure and Domestic Response*. Stanford, CA: Stanford University Press, 1967.
Heller, Francis H., and John R. Gillingham, eds. *NATO: The Founding of the Atlantic Alliance and the Integration of Europe*. New York: St. Martin's Press, 1992.
Hellmann, Gunther, and Reinhard Wolf. "Neorealism, Neoliberal Institutionalism, and the Future of NATO," *Security Studies* 3 (1993), pp. 3-43.
Hoffman, Mark. "Critical Theory and the Inter-paradigm Debate," pp. 60-86 in Hugh C. Dyer and Leon Mangasarian, eds., *The Study of International Relations. The State of the Art*. New York: St. Martin's Press, 1989.
Holmes, Kim R. "New World Disorder: A Critique of the United Nations," *Journal of International Affairs* 46 (1993), pp. 323-40.
Hopf, Ted. "Managing the Post-Soviet Security Space: A Continuing Demand for Behavioral Regimes," *Security Studies* 4 (1994/95), pp. 242-80.
Hyland, William G. "America's new course," *Foreign Affairs* 69 (1990), pp. 1-2.
Ikenberry, John. "Conclusion: an institutional approach to American foreign economic policy," *International Organization* 42 (1988), pp. 219-43.
James, Alan. *Peacekeeping in International Politics*. Houndmills: Macmillan, 1990.
Johansen, Robert C. "Toward a New Code of International Conduct: War, Peacekeeping, and Global Constitutionalism," pp. 39-54 in Richard A. Falk, Robert C. Johansen, and Samuel S. Kim, eds., *The Constitutional Foundations of World Peace*. Albany, NJ: State University of New York Press, 1993.
Johnsen, William, and Thomas-Durell Young. *Preparing for the NATO Summit: What are the Pivotal Issues?* Carlisle, PA: U.S. Army War College, Strategic Studies Institute, 1993.
——. *French Policy Toward NATO: Enhanced Selectivity, Vice Rapprochement*. Carlisle, PA: U.S. Army War College, Strategic Studies Institute, 1994.
Katzenstein, Peter, ed. *The Culture of National Security*. New York: Columbia University Press, 1996.
Kegley, Charles W., ed. *Controversies in International Relations Theory. Realism and the Neoliberal Challenge*. New York: St. Martin's Press, 1995.
Kegley, Charles W., and Gregory A. Raymond. *A Multipolar Peace? Great-Power Politics in the Twenty-first Century*. New York: St. Martin's Press, 1994.
Kennan, George F. "Diplomacy in the modern world," pp. 28-31 in John A. Vasquez, ed., *Classics of International Relations*. 3. Ed. Upper Saddle River, NJ: Prentice Hall, 1996.
Keohane, Robert O. *After Hegemony. Cooperation and Discord in the World Political Economy*. Princeton, NJ: Princeton University Press, 1984.
——. *International Institutions and State Power. Essays in International Relations Theory*. Boulder, CO: Westview, 1989.
——. "The Analysis of International Regimes. Toward a European-American Research Programme," pp. 23-45 in Volker Rittberger, ed., *Regime Theory and International Relations*. Oxford: Clarendon, 1993.
——. "Institutional Theory and the Realist Challenge after the Cold War," pp. 269-300 in David A. Baldwin, ed., *Neorealism and Neoliberalism. The Contemporary Debate*. New York: Columbia University Press, 1993.
Keohane, Robert O., and Lisa L. Martin. "The Promise of Institutionalist Theory," *International Security* 20 (1995), No. 1, pp. 39-51.

Kielinger, Thomas, and Max Otte. "Germany: the pressured power," *Foreign Policy*, No. 91 (1993), pp. 44-62.

Klare, Michael T., and Daniel C. Thomas, eds. *World Security. Challenges for a New Century*. 2. Ed., New York: St. Martin's Press, 1994.

Klein, Bradley S. "After Strategy: The Search for a Post-Modern Politics of Peace," *Alternatives* 13 (1988), pp. 293-318.

——. "How the West was One: Representational Politics of NATO," *International Studies Quarterly* 34 (1990), pp. 311-25.

——. *Strategic Studies and World Order.* Cambridge: Cambridge University Press, 1994.

Kober, Stanley. "Idealpolitik," *Foreign Policy*, No. 79 (1990), pp. 3-24.

Koelble, Thomas A. "The new institutionalism in political science and sociology," *Comparative Politics* 27 (1995), pp. 231-43.

Koslowski, Rey, and Friedrich V. Kratochwil. "Understanding change in international politics: the Soviet empire's demise and the international system," *International Organization* 48 (1994), pp. 215-47.

Krasner, Stephen D. "Structural causes and regime consequences: regimes as intervening variables," pp. 1-21 in Stephen D. Krasner, ed., *International Regimes.* Ithaca, NY: Cornell University Press, 1983.

Krause, Keith, and Michael C. Williams. "Broadening the agenda of security studies: Politics and methods," *Mershon International Studies Review* 40 (1996), pp. 229-54.

Laird, Robbin F. "The West Europeans and peace-keeping," pp. 107-21 in James Cooney et. al., eds., *Deutsch-Amerikanische Beziehungen, Jahrbuch 2.* Frankfurt/M.: Campus, 1994.

Lapid, Yosef, and Friedrich Kratochwil, eds. *The Return of Culture and Identity in IR Theory.* Boulder, CO: Rienner, 1996.

Last, David, and David B. Carment. "Conflict prevention and internal conflict," summary of a workshop held at Carleton University, Ontario, 8 March 1995.

Laursen, Finn. "The Common Foreign and Security Policy of the European Union: Words or Deeds?" pp. 153-77 in Ingo Peters, ed., *New Security Challenges. The Adaptation of International Institutions. Reforming the UN, NATO, EU and CSCE Since 1989.* New York: St. Martin's Press, 1995.

Layne, Christopher. "Kant or Cant. The Myth of Democratic Peace," *International Security* 19 (1994), No. 2, pp. 5-49.

Lebow, Richard Ned. "The long peace, the end of the cold war, and the failure of realism," *International Organization* 48 (1994), pp. 249-77.

Lebow, Richard Ned, and Thomas Risse-Kappen, eds. *International Relations Theory and the End of the Cold War.* New York: Columbia University Press, 1995.

Le Gloannec, Anne-Marie. "The implications of German unification for Western Europe," pp. 251-78 in Paul B. Stares, ed., *The New Germany and the New Europe.* Washington, D.C.: Brookings, 1992.

Levine, Robert A. *NATO, the Subjective Alliance: The Debate Over the Future.* Santa Monica, CA: RAND, 1988.

——. "The United States," pp. 13-29 in Robert A. Levine, ed., *Transition and Turmoil in the Atlantic Alliance.* New York: Crane Russak, 1992.

Levine, Robert A., ed. *Transition and Turmoil in the Atlantic Alliance.* New York: Crane Russak, 1992.

Lider, Julian. *Origins and Development of West German Military Thought.* Vol. 1: *1949-1966.* Aldershot: Gower, 1986.

———. *Origins and Development of West German Military Thought.* Vol. 2: *1966-1988.* Aldershot: Gower, 1988.

Lieber, Robert J. "Existential Realism After the Cold War," *Washington Quarterly* 16 (1993), No. 1, pp. 155-68.

Lipschutz, Ronnie D., ed. *On Security.* New York: Columbia University Press, 1995.

Little, Richard. "International Relations and the Methodological Turn," *Political Studies* 39 (1991), pp. 463-78.

Livingston, Robert G. "United Germany: bigger and better," *Foreign Policy*, No. 85 (1992), pp. 157-74.

Luke, Timothy W. "Discourses of Disintegration, Texts of Transformation: Re-Reading Realism in the New World Order," *Alternatives* 18 (1993), pp. 229-58.

Lundestad, Geir, and Arne Westad, eds. *Beyond the Cold War: New Dimensions in International Relations.* Oslo: Scandinavian University Press, 1993.

Mackinlay, John. "Improving Multifunctional Forces," *Survival* 36 (1994), No. 3, pp. 149-73.

Mansbach, Richard W. "The World Turned Upside Down," *Journal of East-Asian Affairs* 7 (1993), pp. 451-97.

———. "Neo-This and Neo-That: Or, 'Play It Sam' (Again and Again)," *Mershon International Studies Review* 40 (1996), pp. 90-5.

March, James G., and Johan P. Olsen. *Rediscovering Institutions. The Organizational Basis of Politics.* New York: The Free Press, 1989.

———. *Institutional Perspectives on Political Institutions.* Oslo: The Research Council of Norway, 1994.

Maynes, Charles W. "America without cold war," *Foreign Policy*, No. 78 (1990), pp. 3-25.

———. "A workable Clinton doctrine," *Foreign Policy*, No. 93 (1993/94), pp. 3-20.

McCalla, Robert. "NATO's persistence after the cold war," *International Organization* 50 (1996), pp. 445-75.

McSweeny, Bill. "Identity and Security: Buzan and the Copenhagen School," *Review of International Studies* 22 (1996), pp. 81-93.

Mearsheimer, John J. "Back to the Future. Instability in Europe After the Cold War," *International Security* 15 (1990), No. 1, pp. 5-56.

———. "The False Promise of International Institutions," *International Security* 19 (1994/95), No. 3, pp. 5-49.

Meiers, Franz-Josef. *NATO's Peacekeeping Dilemma.* Bonn: Europa Union Verlag, 1996.

Menon, Anand. "From independence to cooperation: France, NATO and European security," *International Affairs* (London) 71 (1995), pp. 19-34.

Miller, Lynn H. *Global Order. Values and Power in International Politics.* 3. Ed. Boulder, CO: Westview, 1994.

Miller, Paul D. *Retaining Alliance Relevancy. NATO and the Combined Joint Task Force Concept.* Cambridge, MA: Institute for Foreign Policy Analysis, 1994.

Milner, Helen. "International Theories of Cooperation Among Nations. Strengths and Weaknesses," *World Politics* 44 (1992), pp. 466-96.

Moens, Alexander. "The Formative Years of the New NATO: Diplomacy from London to Rome," pp. 24-47 in Alexander Moens and Christopher Anstis, eds., *Disconcerted Europe. The Search for a New Security Architecture.* Boulder, CO: Westview, 1994.

Moravcsik, Andrew. "Introduction. Integrating International and Domestic Theories of International Bargaining," pp. 3-42 in Peter B. Evans, Harold K. Jacobson and Robert

D. Putnam, eds., *Double-Edged Diplomacy. International Bargaining and Domestic Politics.* Berkeley: University of California Press, 1993.

Morgan, Patrick. "Multilateralism and Security: Prospects in Europe," pp. 327-64 in John G. Ruggie, ed., *Multilateralism Matters. The Theory and Praxis of an Institutional Form.* New York: Columbia University Press, 1993.

Morgenthau, Hans J. *Scientific Man vs. Power Politics.* Chicago: Chicago University Press, 1946.

Morgenthau, Hans J., and Kenneth W. Thompson. *Politics Among Nations. The Struggle for Power and Peace.* 6. Ed. New York: Knopf, 1985.

Naumann, Klaus. *Die Bundeswehr in einer Welt im Umbruch.* Berlin: Siedler, 1994.

Nerlich, Uwe. "Deutsche Sicherheitspolitik und Konflikte außerhalb des NATO-Gebiets," *Europa-Archiv* 46 (1991), pp. 303-10.

———. "Neue Sicherheitsfunktionen der NATO," in *Europa-Archiv* 48 (1993), pp. 663-72.

Neville-Jones, Pauline. "Dayton, IFOR and Alliance Relations in Bosnia," *Survival* 38 (1996), No. 4, pp. 45-65.

Nye, Joseph S. "American power and a post-cold war world," pp. 33-54 in *Facing the Future: American Strategy in the 1990s.* Lanham, ML: Aspen Institute, 1991.

O'Hanlon, Michael. "Transforming NATO: The Role of European Forces," *Survival* 39 (1997), No. 3, pp. 5-15.

Onuf, Nicholas G. *The World of Our Making. Rules and Rule in Social Theory.* Columbia, SC: University of South Carolina Press, 1989.

Papacosma, S. Victor, and Mary Ann Heiss, eds. *NATO in the Post-Cold War Era: Does It Have a Future?* New York: St. Martin's Press, 1995.

Peters, Ingo, ed. *New Security Challenges: The Adaptation of International Institutions. Reforming the UN, NATO, EU and CSCE Since 1989.* New York: St. Martin's Press, 1996.

Posen, Barry R. "Security Dilemma and Ethnic Conflict," pp. 103-24 in Michael E. Brown, ed., *Ethnic Conflict and International Security.* Princeton, NJ: Princeton University Press, 1993.

Powell, Robert. "Anarchy in international relations theory: the neorealist-neoliberal debate," *International Organization* 48 (1994), pp. 313-44.

Powell, Walter W., and Paul J. DiMaggio, eds. *The New Institutionalism in Organizational Analysis.* Chicago, IL: University of Chicago Press, 1991.

Ray, James Lee, and Bruce Russett. "The Future as Arbiter of Theoretical Controversies: Predictions, Explanations and the End of the Cold War," *British Journal of Political Science* 26 (1996), pp. 441-70.

Reid, Escott. *Time of Fear and Hope. The Making of the North Atlantic Treaty 1947-1949.* Toronto: McClelland and Stewart, 1977.

Rengger, Nicholas J. "No longer 'A Tournament of Distinctive Knights'? Systemic Transition and the Priority of International Order," pp. 145-74 in Mike Bowker and Richard Brown, eds., *From War to Collapse: Theory and World Politics in the 1980s.* Cambridge: Cambridge University Press, 1993.

Righter, Rosemary. *Utopia Lost. The United Nations and World Order.* New York: Twentieth Century Fund Press, 1995.

Risse-Kappen, Thomas, ed. *Bringing Transnational Relations Back In. Non-State Actors, Domestic Structures and International Institutions.* New York: Columbia University Press, 1995.

Rittberger, Volker, and Michael Zürn. "Transformation der Konflikte in den Ost-West-Beziehungen. Versuch einer institutionalistischen Bestandsaufnahme," *Politische Vierteljahresschrift* 32 (1991), pp. 399-424.
Rochester, J. Martin. "The United Nations in a New World Order: Reviving the Theory and Practice of International Organization," pp. 199-221 in Charles W. Kegley, ed., *Controversies in International Relations Theory. Realism and the Neoliberal Challenge*. New York: St. Martin's Press, 1995.
Rosenau, James N., and Ernst-Otto Czempiel, eds. *Governance Without Government: Order and Change in World Politics*. Cambridge: Cambridge University Press, 1992.
Rosenberg, Justin. *The Empire of Civil Society. A Critique of the Realist Theory of International Relations*. London: Verso, 1994.
Ruggie, John G., ed. *Multilateralism Matters. The Theory and Praxis of an Institutional Form*. New York: Columbia University Press, 1993.
Russett, Bruce. *Grasping the Democratic Peace. Principles for a Post-Cold War World*. Princeton, NJ: Princeton University Press, 1993.
Ryan, Stephen. *Ethnic Conflict and International Relations*. Aldershot: Dartmouth, 1990.
Scharpf, Fritz W. "Die Handlungsfähigkeit des Staates am Ende des zwanzigsten Jahrhunderts," *Politische Vierteljahresschrift* 32 (1991), pp. 621-34.
Schlör, Wolfgang F. *German Security Policy. An Examination of the Trends in German Security Policy in a New European and Global Context*. London: IISS, 1993.
Schmidt, Peter. "The Evolution of European Security Structures: Master Plan or Trial and Error?" pp. 145-66 in David G. Haglund, ed., *From Euphoria to Hysteria. Western European Security After the Cold War*. Boulder, CO: Westview, 1993.
———. *Germany, France and NATO*. Carlisle, PA: U.S. Army War College, Strategic Studies Institute, 1994.
Scholte, Jan Aart. *International Relations of Social Change*. Buckingham, PA: Open University Press, 1993.
Scott, Bruce. "NATO after Iraq: Out of Sector, or Out of Business?" *European Security* 2 (1993), pp. 227-43.
Seabury, Paul. *Power, Freedom and Diplomacy*. New York: Random House, 1963.
Seydoux, Alexis, and Jérôme Paolini. "From Interblocking to Institutional Evolutionism," pp. 171-202 in European Strategy Group, ed., *Challenges and Responses to Future European Security: British, French and German Perspectives*. N.p., 1993.
Shapiro, Michael J. *Reading the Postmodern Polity. Political Theory as Textual Practice*. Minneapolis, MN: University of Minnesota Press, 1992.
Siedschlag, Alexander. *Die aktive Beteiligung Deutschlands an militärischen Aktionen zur Verwirklichung Kollektiver Sicherheit*. Frankfurt/M.: Peter Lang, 1995.
———. "Deutsche Außenpolitik im Dilemma der doppelten Normilität," *Jahrbuch für Politik* 5 (1995), pp. 297-318.
———. "Peaceful Settlement of Disputes and Conflict Management in Areas of ethnonational Tension," pp. 35-56 in Jörg Calließ and Christine M. Merkel, eds., *Peaceful Settlement of Conflicts as a Joint Task for International Organizations, Governments and Civil Society*. Vol. 1. Rehburg-Loccum: Evangelische Akademie Loccum, 1995.
———. *Neorealismus, Neoliberalismus und postinternationale Politik*. Opladen: Westdeutscher Verlag, 1997.
Sloan, Stanley R., ed. *NATO in the 1990s*. Washington, D.C.: Pergamon-Brassey's, 1989.
Snyder, Glenn H. "The Security Dilemma in Alliance Politics," *World Politics* 36 (1984), pp. 461-95.

———. "Alliance Theory: A Neorealist First Cut," *Journal of International Affairs* 44 (1990), pp. 103-23.

Stein, George. "The Euro-Corps and Future European Security Architecture," *European Security* 2 (1993), pp. 200-26.

Steinberg, James B. *Overlapping Institutions, Underinsured Security: The Evolution of the Post-Cold War Security Order*. Santa Monica, CA, RAND, 1993.

Stuart, Douglas, and William Tow. *The Limits of Alliance. NATO Out-of-Area Problems Since 1949*. Baltimore, MD: Johns Hopkins University Press, 1990.

Summers, Harry. "What is War," *Harpers* 268 (1984), No. 1608, pp. 75-8.

Szabo, Stephen F. *The Changing Politics of German Security*. New York: St. Martin's Press, 1990.

"The Western European Union in the 1990s: Searching for a Role," Strategic Outreach Conference Report, U.S. Army War College, Strategic Studies Institute, Carlisle, PA, 1993.

Wæver, Ole. "Securitization and Desecuritization," pp. 46-86 in Ronnie D. Lipschutz, ed., *On Security*. New York: Columbia University Press, 1995.

Wæver, Ole, Pierre Lemaitre, and Elzbieta Tromer, eds. *European Polyphony: Perspectives Beyond East-West Confrontation*. New York: St. Martin's Press, 1989.

Wagner, R. Harrison. "What was bipolarity?" *International Organization* 47 (1993), pp. 77-106.

Wallace, William. "European-Atlantic Security Institutions: Current State and Future Prospects," *International Spectator* 29 (1994), No. 3, pp. 37-51.

Wallensteen, Peter, and Margareta Sollenberg. "After the Cold War: Emerging Patterns of Armed Conflict 1989-94," *Journal of Peace Research* 32 (1995), pp. 345-60.

Wallop, Malcolm. "America needs a post-containment doctrine," *Orbis* 37 (1993), pp. 187-203.

Waltz, Kenneth N. *Theory of International Politics*. New York: McGraw-Hill, 1979.

———. "Reflections on Theory of International Politics: A Response to My Critics," pp. 322-45 in Robert O. Keohane, ed., *Neorealism and Its Critics*. New York: Columbia University Press, 1986.

———. "The Emerging Structure of International Politics," *International Security* 18 (1993), No. 2, pp. 44-79.

Weber, Steve. "Does NATO have a future?" pp. 360-95 in Beverly Crawford, ed., *The Future of European Security*. Berkeley, CA: University of California Press, 1992.

Weiss, Thomas G., ed. *Collective Security in a Changing World*. Boulder, CO: Rienner, 1993.

Wendt, Alexander. "The Agent-Structure Problem in International Relations Theory," *International Organization* 4 (1987), No. 3, pp. 335-70.

———. "Constructing International Politics," *International Security* 20 (1995), No. 1, pp. 71-81.

Wendt, Alexander, and Raymond Duvall. "Institutions and International Order," pp. 51-73 in Ernst-Otto Czempiel and James N. Rosenau, eds., *Global Changes and Theoretical Challenges. Approaches to World Politics for the 1990s*. Lexington, MA: Lexington Books, 1989.

Yost, David S. "France and the Gulf War of 1990-1991. Political-military lessons learned," *Journal of Strategic Studies* 16 (1993), pp. 339-74.

Young, Thomas-Durell. "German national command structures after unification: A new German general staff?" *Armed Forces and Society* 22 (1996), pp. 379-417.

Zacher, Mark W. "Toward a Theory of International Regimes," *Journal of International Affairs* 44 (1990), pp. 139-57.

Zelikow, Philip. "Foreign Policy Engineering: From Theory to Practice and Back Again," *International Security* 18 (1994), No. 4, pp. 143-71.

Politikwissenschaft

Egbert Scheunemann
Ökologisch-Humane Wirtschaftsdemokratie
Teil C: Ökologische Kritik am Industrialismus und sozialökologische Alternativen

Der hier vorliegende Teil C *Ökologische Kritik am Industrialismus und sozialökologische Alternativen* schließt das Gesamtprojekt *Ökologisch-humane Wirtschaftsdemokratie* ab, dessen Teile A/B in diesem Verlag bereits 1990 erschienen. In den ersten beiden Teilen dieses Projektes wurde das theoretische Modell einer *humanen Wirtschaftsdemokratie von Ota Šik* als ein ebenso *umfassendes* wie *detailliertes* und *wissenschaftlich fundiertes* gesellschaftliches Alternativmodell zusammenfassend dargestellt und konstruktiv kritisiert. In diesem dritten Teil wird der (1990 schon angekündigte) Versuch unternommen, dieses Modell einer *humanen Wirtschaftsdemokratie* zu dem einer *ökologisch-humanen Wirtschaftsdemokratie* zu erweitern.
Dabei soll *erstens* aufgezeigt werden, daß das kapitalistische Industriesystem hochgradig *tautologisch* (selbstbegründend) und/oder *kontraproduktiv* (zerstörerisch) konstruiert ist. Das *Verkehrssystem Automobil* beispielsweise bringt in der Summe *aller* einzel- wie volkswirtschaftlichen Zeitaufwendungen und Zeitgewinne nicht nur *keinerlei Beschleunigung über die menschliche Gehgeschwindigkeit hinaus*, sondern es *verlangsamt* uns – und es tötet in der BRD jährlich knapp *zehntausend* Menschen, verletzt *hunderttausende* und zerstört unsere Umwelt wie unsere Städte als soziale Lebensräume. Nicht ganz so katastrophal, aber ähnlich tautologisch und kontraproduktiv fallen die zeitökonomischen wie ökosozialen Bilanzen des industriellen *Energiesystems* wie der der industriellen *Landwirtschaft* aus. Das Industriesystem ist, wie hier ebenso empirisch fundiert wie analytisch stringent aufgezeigt wird, in einer Größenordnung von etwa *zwei Dritteln* tautologisch und/oder ökosozial kontraproduktiv – und d. h. umgangssprachlich formuliert: *idiotisch* und *menschenverachtend* – konstruiert.
In einem *zweiten* Schritt soll aufgezeigt werden, mit welchen mikro- und makroökonomischen sowie ökologischen bzw. umweltpolitischen Konzepten und Maßnahmen das Industriesystem auf seinen *rational begründbaren* Kern *reduziert* und wie dieser produktive Kern möglichst *ökologisch und sozial verträglich* gestaltet werden kann.
Sowohl die hier geleistete *Kritik* am Industriesystem wie die Auswahl und Konstruktion *alternativer Konzepte* orientieren sich am Projekt *Humanismus und Aufklärung* als regulativer Idee politischen Handelns: Das produktive *Reich der Notwendigkeit* soll so weit wie möglich *reduziert* werden zugunsten einer maximalen Erweiterung des *Reiches der Freiheit* als Grundlage einer umfassenden sinnlichen, erotischen, humanen, sozialen, kulturellen, künstlerischen und wissenschaftlichen Entfaltung des Menschen. Wenn man das Projekt *Humanismus und Aufklärung* identifiziert mit dem Projekt der *Moderne*, dann erscheint diese Moderne – jenseits aller vielpublizierten postmodern-zeitgeistigen Geistlosigkeiten – gerade mal schüchtern begonnen zu haben.
Bd. 31, 1995, 840 S., 88,80 DM, br.,
ISBN 3–8258–2612–0

Tesfaye Tafesse
Villagization in Northern Shewa, Ethiopia: Impact Assessment
Bd. 32, 1995, 160 S., 38,80 DM*, br.,
ISBN 3-8258-2618-X

Volker Hildebrandt
Epochenumbruch in der Moderne
Eine Kontroverse zwischen Robert Kurz und Ulrich Beck

Allerorten unbestritten befindet sich die Gesellschaft, die vor 200 Jahren mit den politischen Revolutionen in Frankreich und Amerika sowie mit der industriellen Revolution Englands ihren Ausgang nahm, in einem dramatischen Umbruch. Auf dem Höhepunkt ihrer innergesellschaftlichen und globalen Durchsetzung erlebt die gemeiniglich als Moderne begriffene Gesellschaft unserer Tage eine schlechterdings nicht für möglich gehaltene Krise. Strittig und zu klären ist, wie die gegenwärtigen Umbrüche einzuordnen sind. Zwei Grundlinien der Diskussion schälen sich heraus: größerer Strukturwandel einer in ihren Fundamenten unangetasteten Moderne versus epochaler Bruch mit der gesamten Modernisierungsgeschichte.
Zur Klärung dieser Metastreitfrage aller aktuellen gesellschaftspolitischen Diskussionen ist Theoriearbeit und begriffliches Denken gefordert. Auf diesen Pfaden werden erstmalig zwei exponierte und dabei grundverschiedene Theoretiker des Epochenbruchs, Robert Kurz und Ulrich Beck, zueinander in Beziehung gesetzt und konfrontiert mit den Essentials des landläufigen Modernisierungsdiskurses, der in der Moderne das "Ende der Geschichte" erblickt. Dem vielbeschworenen "Ende der Großtheorien" wird in dieser Arbeit eine klare Absage erteilt, ohne dabei auf steinerne Theorieableitungen zurückzugreifen.
Die bezüglich theoretischer Breite umfassend angelegte Abhandlung wird darüber hinaus durch umfängliche Primärquellen komplettiert (fast ein Drittel des Umfangs). Im Anhang liegen Interviews sowohl mit dem Fundamentalkritiker der Arbeitsgesellschaft, Robert Kurz, als auch mit dem Vertreter der Risikogesellschaftstheorie, Ulrich Beck, vor. Durch diese erstmals veröffentlichten Interviews

LIT Verlag Münster – Hamburg – London
Bestellungen über: Dieckstr. 73 48145 Münster Tel.: 0251 – 23 50 91 Fax: 0251 – 23 19 72
* unverbindliche Preisempfehlung

ist eine dialogische Form der Theorienauseinandersetzung möglich: zum einen, weil den beiden Theoretikern die Forschungskonzeption vorweg bekannt war und der Interviewer den Interviewverlauf auch auf die vom jeweils anderen Großtheoretiker stärker berücksichtigten Problemebenen lenken konnte; zum anderen, weil der Leser die begrifflich erarbeiteten Ergebnisse des Autors mit Originalstellungnahmen der vieldiskutierten Theoretiker konfrontieren kann.
Bd. 33, 1996, 184 S., 34,80 DM, br.,
ISBN 3–8258–2622–8

Michael Schmidt
Die FDP und die deutsche Frage
1949–1990
Die FDP war bereits in den fünfziger und sechziger Jahren eine Partei mit unbestreitbarer deutschlandpolitischer Kompetenz. Ab 1966 wurden der FDP entscheidende Weichenstellungen für eine neue Deutschlandpolitik gestellt, deren Umsetzung in der sozial-liberalen Koalition erfolgte. Die deutsche Teilung sollte in der langfristigen Zielperspektive einer europäischen Friedensordnung aufgehoben werden. Nach 1982 war die FDP Garant dafür, daß die mit den Sozialdemokraten begonnene neue Deutschland- und Ostpolitik auch mit den Unionsparteien weitergeführt werden konnte. Am Prozeß der deutschen Einigung war die FDP maßgeblich beteiligt. Vor allem das Verhandlungsgeschick von Hans-Dietrich Genscher bei den Zwei-plus-Vier-Verhandlungen trug maßgeblich mit zur Regelung der äußeren Aspekte der deutschen Einheit und damit zur Lösung der deutschen Frage bei.
Bd. 34, 1995, 352 S., 68,80 DM, br.,
ISBN 3–8258–2631–7

Andreas Pihan
Politiksequenzen der Pflegeversicherung
Zur Bedeutung von Politiknetzwerken
Dieses Buch beschäftigt sich mit dem Thema Pflegeversicherung aus politikwissenschaftlicher Sicht. Es gibt einen Überblick über die in 20jähriger Diskussion gemachten Vorschläge zur Pflegefrage. Hierbei wird der Diskussionsverlauf mit Hilfe des policy cycle rekonstruiert und in charakteristische Sequenzen eingeteilt. Im Zusammenhang mit der Sequenzeinteilung gibt der neuerdings in der Politikwissenschaft diskutierte Netzwerkansatz über die in der Pflegedebatte vorgefundenen Akteurskonstellationen Auskunft.
Bd. 35, 1996, 200 S., 38,80 DM, br.,
ISBN 3–8258–2828–x

Norbert Kadner
Die größten Klöpse
Bd. 36, 1996, 112 S., 29,80 DM, br.,
ISBN 3–8258–2846–8

Ulrich Schneckener
Das Recht auf Selbstbestimmung
Ethno-nationale Konflikte und internationale Politik
Das Recht auf Selbstbestimmung gehört zu den Grundprinzipien internationaler Politik. Doch was verbirgt sich dahinter? Wer ist das "Selbst" bei Selbstbestimmung? Wer hat wann einen Anspruch darauf, seine Angelegenheiten selbst zu bestimmen? Welche Rolle spielt dieses Prinzip im Verhältnis zu anderen Normen der internationalen Staatenwelt? Vor dem Hintergrund zunehmender ethnonationaler Konflikte nach Ende des Kalten Krieges stellen sich diese Fragen – wie bereits nach 1918 und nach 1945 – mit neuer Dringlichkeit.
Bd. 37, 1996, 168 S., 29,80 DM, br.,
ISBN 3-8258-2862-x

Willi Göttert
Friedensschutzplan zur Kriegsabschaffung
Friedensrecht bricht Kriegsgewalt
Wer will, kann mit dem hier dokumentierten konkreten Plan Frieden wahren und den Krieg abschaffen. Dieses Buch informiert über die "Zivilen" über diese Möglichkeit, nachdem unsere Politiker und Militärs in Bonn schon im Januar 1995 dieses friedenschaffende Instrumentarium erhalten haben, wo es noch auf Eis liegt. Der damals an sie gerichtete Antrag gilt auch der übrigen Bevölkerung Deutschlands: "Die Rüsselsheimer Friedensinitiative beantragt, den beiliegenden Konventions-Entwurf für umfassende Abrüstung und geschützten Weltfrieden dahingehend zu prüfen, ob er geeignet ist, den "Willen des deutschen Volkes zu erfüllen, dem Frieden Europas und der Welt zu dienen". (Präambel GG). Bei seiner Anwendung kann der Friede bewahrt und der Krieg durch die Abrüstung aller Kriegswaffen abgeschafft werden. – Wir fügen diesem Antrag ein "weiterführendes Weißbuch 1994" bei, in dem wir darstellen, wie es möglich ist, falls die Konvention in die deutsche Friedenspolitik integriert wird, daß Deutschland am weltweiten Friedensschutz teilnehmen und mithelfen kann, den dauerhaft geschützten Frieden für Europa und die Welt zu verwirklichen".
Erstmals wird hier, was bisher als Utopie und Illusion galt, als ein gangbarer Weg für ein machbares Friedensziel aufgezeigt, bei dem kein paradiesischer Friede, sondern der uns bekannte und täglich ausgeübte Rechtsfriede in den Kommunen des Rechtsstaates Deutschlands Pate steht.
Die Autoren dieses konkreten, hier dokumentierten Plans für einen echten und haltbaren Rechtsfrieden der Zukunft hoffen darauf, daß sich die deutschen Staatsverantwortlichen "oben" und wir Bürger-

LIT Verlag Münster – Hamburg – London
Bestellungen über: Dieckstr. 73 48145 Münster Tel.: 0251–23 50 91 Fax: 0251–23 19 72
∗ unverbindliche Preisempfehlung

verantwortlichen "unten" für diesen Kampf Pro Frieden Contra Krieg verbünden und ihn konkret im "Heute und Hier" beginnen.
Bd. 38, 1998, 320 S., 38,80 DM*, br.,
ISBN 3-8258-2954-5

Elmar Bieber
Der Euthanasiebefehl Hitlers in der Bewertung rechtspositivistischer Theorien
Vielfach wird pauschal angenommen, daß der Rechtspositivismus gegenüber staatlichem Unrecht wehrlos oder indifferent ist. Dieser Vorwurf wird in der Literatur jedoch selten konkret belegt.
Der Autor unternimmt es daher anhand eines Einzelfalles, nämlich dem sogenannten Euthanasiebefehls Hitlers, diese These auf ihren Richtigkeitsgehalt zu überprüfen.
Untersucht werden Ansätze repräsentativer Vertreter des sogenannten etatistischen (z. B. Kelsen), soziologischen (Geiger) und psychologischen Rechtspositivismus (z. B. Jellinek).
Dabei vermittelt das Buch u. a. zugleich wichtige Einblicke in das exemplarische Wirken des sog. Doppelstaates im NS-Staat.
Der ausgewählte Analyseansatz läßt sich zudem, wie der Verfasser zum Schluß noch andeutet, auch für die Aufarbeitung der DDR-Vergangenheit (insbesondere für die Mauerschützenproblematik) fruchtbar machen.
Bd. 39, 1996, 152 S., 34,80 DM, br.,
ISBN 3–8258–3010–1

Wilhelm M. Stirn
Katastrophenhilfe in Entwicklungsländern
Effizienzpotentiale der deutschen Auslandshilfe
Natur- und Kulturkatastrophen in Entwicklungsländern fordern zunehmend menschliche Opfer und verursachen steigende materielle Schäden. Medienberichte aus den Katastrophengebieten führen jedes Jahr in Deutschland zu privaten und staatlichen Spenden in Höhe von mehreren hundert Millionen DM. Aber: Hilft unsere Hilfe wirklich? Hält Sie das Versprechen, "humanitäre Hilfe" zu sein?
Die vorliegende Arbeit widmet sich einem hochaktuellen Thema. Sie analysiert die Hilfen und Verhaltensweisen der einzelnen beteiligten Akteure und untersucht die tatsächliche Effizienz der deutschen Auslandshilfe.
Die Ergebnisse sind überraschend. Die aufgezeigten Problemlösungsansätze gilt es in die Praxis umzusetzen, soll ein humanitärer Anspruch in höherem Maße als bisher eingelöst werden.
Bd. 40, 1996, 384 S., 48,80 DM, br.,
ISBN 3–8258–3011–x

Florian Raunig
Herrschaft ohne Grenzen?
Der individuelle Freiraum als Parameter totalitärer Herrschaft
Vorliegender Band geht der Frage nach, ob und inwieweit der Mensch als Individuum und eigenständige Persönlichkeit "total" beherrscht werden kann. Mittels eines machttheoretischen, politologisch-philosophischen Ansatzes werden aus der Perspektive des herrschaftsunterworfenen Individuums Wirkungen und Konsequenzen totalitärer Herrschaft erschlossen. Als entscheidendes Kriterium erweisen sich dabei die individuellen Freiräume: sowohl bei der theoretischen Ergründung der Bedeutungsgehalte von "total" und "totalitär" als auch bei der Konfrontation der theoretischen Erkenntnisse mit konkreten Herrschaftstypen und historischen Herrschaftssystemen.
Die Untersuchung schließt mit einem kurzen Essay zu potentiellen, totalitären Gefahren der Gentechnologie sowie Zusammenfassungen in englischer, französischer und italienischer Sprache.
Bd. 41, 1997, 168 S., 38,80 DM*, br.,
ISBN 3-8258-3136-1

Roland Kühnel
Integrismus versus Integration?
Sprachloyalität und linguistical correctness von Marokkanern in Brüssel
Sprachloyalität und linguistical correctness sind als wesentliche Kriterien von Staatsloyalität und political correctness von besonderer Relevanz. Dies gilt gerade für in Europa lebende nichteuropäische und nichtchristliche allochthone Bevölkerungsgruppen. Die vorliegende Studie untersucht am Beispiel der Marokkaner in Brüssel die Interdependenz von Sprachverhalten und Islamität bei arabophonen bzw. berberophonen Auslandsmaghrebinern. Dabei wird fokussiert, in welchem Zusammenhang Arabischkenntnisse und eine demonstrative Religiosität stehen und inwieweit die Marokkaner – auch im Vergleich zu Türken und anderen Minderheiten – bereits heute eine normative Kraft in Belgien darstellen. Eine Umfrage unter 300 Migranten und eine Analyse der arabischen Medien in Brüssel zeigen potentielle Auswirkungen von Sprachwechsel (code-switching Arabisch-Französisch) und Identitätswechsel auf eine multiethnische Zukunft Westeuropas. Brüssel mit dem Anspruch als europäische Hauptstadt könnte dafür Modellcharakter besitzen.
Bd. 42, 1997, 256 S., 48,80 DM*, br.,
ISBN 3-8258-3278-3

LIT Verlag Münster – Hamburg – London
Bestellungen über: Dieckstr. 73 48145 Münster Tel.: 0251 – 23 50 91 Fax: 0251 – 23 19 72

* unverbindliche Preisempfehlung

Jaime Sperberg
Urbane Landbesetzungen in Santiago de Chile und Buenos Aires
Soziale Bewegungen in Chile und Argentinien in den 80er Jahren
Die achtziger Jahre werden in Lateinamerika als das "verlorene Jahrzehnt" bezeichnet. Diese eher auf die negative sozio-ökonomische Entwicklung bezogene Aussage verdeckt aber die in dieser Periode entfalteten Partizipations- und Demokratisierungspotentiale aus der Zivilgesellschaft. Die in den 80er- Jahren in Santiago de Chile und Buenos Aires stattgefundenen Landbesetzungen zur Lösung des Wohnproblems haben sowohl die autoritären Regime beider Länder wie auch die in Argentinien seit 1983 wiedergewonnene Demokratie herausgefordert. Die Betrachtung der Landbesetzungen und ihrer Organisationen, vor dem Hintergrund unterschiedlicher Regimetypen (autoritär versus demokratisch), eröffnen ein komplexes Bild der von den Landbesetzern verfolgten Strategien und der staatlichen Aktionen bzw. Reaktionen. Auch wenn sich zeitweise autonome Landbesetzerbewegungen konstituieren konnten, war die Gefahr einer "Vereinnahmung" durch übergreifende parteipolitische und stark personenorientierte klientelistische Bezüge nicht auszuschließen.
Bd. 43, 1997, 144 S., 39,80 DM*, br.,
ISBN 3-8258-3407-7

Cornelia Rieß
Der überforderte Partner?
Konzepte amerikanischer Deutschlandpolitik nach dem Ende des Ost-West-Konflikts
Bd. 45, 1997, 376 S., 49,80 DM*, br.,
ISBN 3-8258-3413-1

Bert Butz; Sebastian Haunss; Robert Hennies; Martina Richter
Flexible Allrounder: Wege in den Beruf für PolitologInnen
Ergebnisse einer AbsolventInnenbefragung am Institut für Politische Wissenschaft der Universität Hamburg
Welche beruflichen Wege stehen PolitologInnen offen? Was können sie mit ihrem im Studium erworbenen Wissen anfangen?
In zwei Untersuchungen über die beruflichen Werdegänge der AbsolventInnen der Jahre 1970–1992 des Instituts für Politische Wissenschaft der Universität Hamburg gehen die AutorInnen diesen Fragen nach.
Die Ergebnisse zeigen: Das Studium der Politikwissenschaft vermittelt ein Set von Qualifikationen, für das auf dem Arbeitsmarkt durchaus Nachfrage besteht. Allerdings handelt es sich dabei nicht um ein klar umrissenes Qualifikationsprofil. PolitologInnen sind vielmehr flexible Allrounder.
Bd. 46, 1998, 240 S., 49,80 DM*, br.,
ISBN 3-8258-3538-3

Frank Havighorst
Regionalisierung der Regionalpolitik
Bd. 47, 1998, 216 S., 59,80 DM*, br.,
ISBN 3-8258-3636-3

Laurenz Awater
Die politische Wirtschaftsgeschichte der VR China
Vom Sowjetmodell zur sozialistischen Marktwirtschaft
In komprimierter Form wird die wechselvolle wirtschaftspolitische Entwicklung Chinas seit dem Anfang der Fünfziger Jahre mit Antworten nach ihrer historischen Kausalität dargestellt, werden die Reformen mit ihren zentralen Problemen beim Übergang in die sog. "sozialistische Marktwirtschaft" nachgezeichnet. Die einzelnen Modelle und Entwicklungsstufen, wie etwa der maoistische "Große Sprung nach vorn", die Berichtigungskampagne "Laßt Hundert Blumen blühen", der "Steinzeit-Kommunismus", "Drei Jahre Schwerarbeit – 10 000 Jahre Glück", die Politik der "Vier Modernisierungen", die "Große proletarische Kulturrevolution", die "Planifikation" französischen Musters oder die "Theorie vom Aufbau des Sozialismus chinesischer Prägung", sie finden mit Belegen und Tabellen ebenso Berücksichtigung wie die neueren außenwirtschaftlichen Aspekte und der Ausblick in die Zukunft.
Bd. 48, 1998, 608 S., 78,80 DM*, br.,
ISBN 3-8258-3221-x

Marie-Theres Norpoth
Norm und Wirklichkeit
Staat und Verfassung im Werk Ernst Rudolf Hubers
Bd. 49, 1998, 474 S., 89,80 DM*, br.,
ISBN 3-8258-3705-x

Dieter Staas
Nullinflation – Karriere einer fatalen Ideologie
Jahr für Jahr fordert die deutsche Inflationshysterie ihre Opfer in Form steigender Arbeitslosigkeit. Längst dreht sich die Deflationsspirale – zunächst langsam noch, aber doch unerbittlich. Während immer mehr Existenzen in ihren Sog geraten, feiert eine unheilige Allianz aus politischer und ökonomischer Ignoranz den Sieg über die Inflation. Ganz vorn dabei, als Bannerträger des Stabilitätswahns: die Deutsche Bundesbank. Über Jahrzehnte hat sie dazu beigetragen, Wachstums-Chancen zu vernichten und Deutschland und Europa ökonomisch erstarren zu lassen. Nun muß sie ihre Kompetenzen an eine europäische Institution abtreten. Höchste Zeit also, Inflation, Geldpolitik und die Ideologie der Bundesbank einmal aus einer ganz anderen Perspektive zu betrachten.
Bd. 50, 1998, 160 S., 29,80 DM*, br.,
ISBN 3-8258-3235-x

LIT Verlag Münster–Hamburg–London
Bestellungen über: Dieckstr. 73 48145 Münster Tel.: 0251 – 23 50 91 Fax: 0251 – 23 19 72
* unverbindliche Preisempfehlung

Luay Ali
Die deutsch-arabischen Beziehungen von 1949–1965
Nach dem Zweiten Weltkrieg kristallisierten sich neue außenpolitische Konstellationen heraus, die sich in der Teilung Deutschlands und der Gründung des Staates Israel widerspiegelten. Das erschwerte die deutsch-arabischen Nachkriegsbeziehungen. Demzufolge ergeben sich bis 1965 drei Entwicklungsphasen, mit deren Hintergründen, Abläufen und nicht zuletzt Folgen sich diese Arbeit auseinandersetzt:
Die erste Phase ist gekennzeichnet durch die Aufnahme der Verhandlungen der Bundesrepublik mit Israel bis zur Unterzeichnung des Wiedergutmachungsabkommens im Sept. 1952, daraus resultierten arabische Proteste, um möglichst dessen Ratifizierung zu verhindern. Eine zweite Phase begann, als die Bundesrepublik ungeachtet der arabischen Interessen Israel mit Waffen belieferte und als Reaktion darauf Walter Ulbricht in Kairo empfangen wurde. Die dritte und die letzte Phase wurde dadurch bestimmt, daß sich die Bundesrepublik auf den Weg zur Anerkennung Israels machte und somit die arabische Nichtanerkennungspolitik mißachtete, was letztendlich zum Zusammenbruch der deutsch-arabischen Beziehungen im Mai 1965 führte.
Bd. 51, 1998, 280 S., 59,80 DM*, br.,
ISBN 3-8258-3734-3

J. Bellers; G. Hufnagel (Hrsg.)
Grenzen der Macht
Festschrift für Wolfgang Perschel
Bd. 52, 1998, 408 S., 69,80 DM*, br.,
ISBN 3-8258-3828-5

Politikwissenschaftliche Perspektiven
herausgegeben von Prof. Dr. Manfred Mols,
(Johannes Gutenberg-Universität Mainz)

Manfred Mols; Peter Birle
Entwicklungsdiskussion und Entwicklungspraxis in Lateinamerika, Südostasien und Indien
Bd. 1, 1993, 250 S., 34,80 DM, br., ISBN 3-89473-767-4

Gernot Lennert
Die Außenbeziehungen der CARICOM-Staaten
Bd. 2, 1992, 550 S., 88,80 DM, br., ISBN 3-88660-800-x

Hans-Joachim Lauth
Mexiko zwischen traditioneller Herrschaft und Modernisierung
Die Gewerkschaften im Wandel von Politik und Wirtschaft (1964–1988)
Bd. 3, 1992, 700 S., 98,80 DM, br., ISBN 3-88660-717-8

Christoph Wagner
Politik in Uruguay 1984–1990
Probleme der demokratischen Konsolidierung
Bd. 4, 1992, 200 S., 48,80 DM, br., ISBN 3-89473-099-4

Karl-Ernst Pfeifer
Nichtregierungsorganisationen – Protagonisten einer neuen Entwicklungspolitik?
Konzeptionelle Grundlagen der Entwicklungszusammenarbeit deutscher Nichtregierungsorganisationen – verdeutlicht an lateinamerikanischen Beispielen
Bd. 5, 1992, 264 S., 58,80 DM, gb., ISBN 3-89473-413-2

Werner Kremp
In Deutschland liegt unser Amerika
Das sozialdemokratische Amerikabild von den Anfängen der SPD bis zur Weimarer Republik
Bd. 6, 1993, 800 S., 98,80 DM, br., ISBN 3-89473-519-8

Manfred Mols; Manfred Wilhelmy von Wolff; Hernan Gutierrez (Hrsg.)
Regionalismus und Kooperation in Lateinamerika und Südostasien
Ein politikwissenschaftlicher Vergleich
Bd. 7, 1993, 516 S., 58,80 DM, br., ISBN 3-89473-621-6

Martin Brixius
Externe Beeinflussungsfaktoren der Demokratie in Costa Rica
Bd. 8, 1993, 250 S., 34,80 DM, br., ISBN 3-89473-625-9

Christoph Müllerleile
Die Integration der CARICOM-Staaten
Fortschritte und Hindernisse auf dem Weg zur Karibischen Gemeinschaft
Bd. 9, 1993, 500 S., 58,80 DM, br., ISBN 3-89473-756-5

Sabine Fischer
Sowjetisch-kubanische Beziehungen ab 1985
Bd. 10, 1996, 135 S., 34,80 DM, br., ISBN 3-8258-3092-6

LIT Verlag Münster – Hamburg – London
Bestellungen über: Dieckstr. 73 48145 Münster Tel.: 0251-23 50 91 Fax: 0251-23 19 72
* unverbindliche Preisempfehlung

Alexander Siedschlag

NATO Meets the Post-strategic Condition

Politikwissenschaft

Band 53

LIT